Published by

The Naval & Military Press Ltd

Unit 5 Riverside, Brambleside
Bellbrook Industrial Estate
Uckfield, East Sussex
TN22 1QQ England

Tel: +44 (0)1825 749494

www.naval-military-press.com
www.nmarchive.com

NOTES

<small>ON</small>

AUSTRO-HUNGARIAN FUZES.

NOVEMBER, 1917.

**Prepared by the General Staff, War Office,
M.I. 3 (b)**

Naval & Military Press Ltd

APPENDIX.

CONVERSION TABLES.

Yards.	Metres.	Metres.	Yards.	Inches.	Centi-metres.	Centi-metres.	Inch
100	91 ·44	100	109 ·36	1	2 ·54	1	0 ·39
200	182 ·88	200	218 ·72	2	5 ·08	2	0 ·79
300	274 ·32	300	328 ·09	3	7 ·62	3	1 ·18
400	365 ·75	400	437 ·45	4	10 ·16	4	1 ·57
500	457 ·19	500	546 ·81	5	12 ·72	5	1 ·97
600	549 ·	600	656 ·	6	15 ·24	6	2 ·36
700	640 ·	700	765 ·	7	17 ·78	7	2 ·75
800	731 ·	800	875 ·	8	20 ·32	8	3 ·15
900	823 ·	900	984 ·	9	22 ·86	9	3 ·54
1,000	914 ·	1,000	1,094 ·	10	25 ·40	10	3 ·94
1,500	1,372 ·	1,500	1,640 ·	11	27 ·94	11	4 ·33
2,000	1,829 ·	2,000	2,187 ·	12	30 ·48	12	4 ·72
2,500	2,286 ·	2,500	2,734 ·	13	33 ·02	13	5 ·11
3,000	2,743 ·	3,000	3,281 ·	14	35 ·56	14	5 ·51
3,500	3,200 ·	3,500	3,828 ·	15	38 ·10	15	5 ·90
4,000	3,657 ·	4,000	4,374 ·	16	40 ·64	16	6 ·30
4,500	4,115 ·	4,500	4,921 ·	17	43 ·18	17	6 ·69
5,000	4,572 ·	5,000	5,468 ·	18	45 ·72	18	7 ·09
5,500	5,029 ·	5,500	6,015 ·	19	48 ·26	19	7 ·48
6,000	5,486 ·	6,000	6,562 ·	20	50 ·80	20	7 ·87
6,500	5,943 ·	6,500	7,109 ·	21	53 ·34	21	8 ·27
7,000	6,401 ·	7,000	7,655 ·	22	55 ·88	22	8 ·66
7,500	6,858 ·	7,500	8,202 ·	23	58 ·42	23	9 ·06
8,000	7,315 ·	8,000	8,749 ·	24	60 ·96	24	9 ·45
8,500	7,772 ·	8,500	9,296 ·	25	63 ·50	25	9 ·84
9,000	8,229 ·	9,000	9,843 ·	26	66 ·04	26	10 ·24
9,500	8,687 ·	9,500	10,389 ·	27	68 ·58	27	10 ·63
10,000	9,144 ·	10,000	10,936 ·	28	71 ·12	28	11 ·02
10,500	9,601 ·	10,500	11,483 ·	29	73 ·66	29	11 ·41
11,000	10,058 ·	11,000	12,030 ·	30	76 ·20	30	11 ·81
11,500	10,515 ·	11,500	12,577 ·	31	78 ·74	31	12 ·20
12,000	10,972 ·	12,000	13,124 ·	32	81 ·28	32	12 ·60
12,500	11,430 ·	12,500	13,670 ·	33	83 ·82	33	12 ·99
13,000	11,887 ·	13,000	14,217 ·	34	86 ·36	34	13 ·39
13,500	12,344 ·	13,500	14,764 ·	35	88 ·90	35	13 ·79

[Continued on page 3 of cover,

ADDENDUM No. 1.

February, 1918.

AMENDMENTS TO "NOTES ON AUSTRO-HUNGARIAN FUZES."

Page 5—

The following table should be used instead of that given :—

TABLE OF FUZES AND PROJECTILES USED WITH VARIOUS GUNS, HOWITZERS AND MORTARS.

Piece.	Fuzes.	Projectiles.
3·7 cm. Infantry Gun (calibre 37 mm.). *Infanterie Rohrrücklaufgeschütz*	—	*Minengranate*, M. 14 and 15. *Brisantsgranate.* Shrapnel. Star-shell.
3·7 cm. A.A. Gun, M. 14 and 16 (calibre 37 mm.)	—	—
(?) 4·5 cm. Infantry Gun....	—	—
(?) 5·4 cm. A.A. Gun, M. 16 (calibre 54 mm.). (*Schnellfeuersteilgeschütz*)	—	—
(?) 5·6 cm. Mountain Gun, M. (?) (calibre 56 mm.). *Gebirgskanone*	—	—
6 cm. Gun, M. 98 in casemate (calibre 57 mm.). *Kasemattkanone*	M. 98	Powder-filled shell, M. 98.
6 cm. Gun, M. 98, in fixed or movable turret (calibre 57 mm.). *Fahrpanzerkanone*	M. 95 *b* .... —	Shrapnel, M. 98/95. Case-shot.
6 cm. Gun, M. 99, in casemate (calibre 57 mm.).	M. 98	Powder-filled shell, M. 98.
6·5 cm. Italian Mountain Gun	—	—
7 cm. Italian Mountain Gun	—	—
7 cm. Mountain Gun, M. 99, 8, 9 and 15 (16 ?) (calibre 72·5 mm.). *Gebirgskanone*	M. 99, 7 cm. (with gaine) M. 99, 7 cm.	*Ekrasit* shell, M. 99 and 5. Shrapnel, M. 99.

Note.—The more important guns are printed in **heavy type**.

(B 13642) Wt. w. 4383—PP690 2750 2/18 H & S P. 18/139

Piece	Fuzes.	Projectiles.
7 cm. A.A. Gun, L/30 on lorry. K.L.Fa.Kan. *Kraftwagenluftfahrzeugabwehrkanone*	—	—
7 cm. Coast Defence Gun, L/42. *Küstenkanone*	M. 97	Shell, M. 98.
	M, 95a	Shrapnel, M. 98.
7·5 cm. **Mountain Gun, M. 15 (16?) (calibre 75 mm.)**	7 cm., M. 15	Universal shell (*Schrapnellgranate*). Shell. Shrapnel.
7·5 cm. Italian Field Gun (calibre 75 mm.)	—	—
8 cm. Field Gun, M. 5 and 5/8 (calibre 76·5 mm). *Feldkanone*	M. 5 (with gaine) M. 8 (with gaine) M. 8 B .... M. 5	*Ammonal* shell, M. 5 and 8.
8 cm. Fortress Gun, M. 5 and 5/9 (calibre 76·5 mm.) *Minimalschartenkanone*	M. 8 .... M. 8 b	Shrapnel, M. 5 and 8.
	Clockwork	Long H.E.shell,M.14(?)
	E.K.Z. 16	" Blue cross " gas shell.
	E.K.Z. 17	"Yellow cross" gasshell.
8 cm. Gun, M. 2, in turret (calibre mm.). *Senkpanzerkanone*	M. 2	Shrapnel, M. 2. Case-shot.
8 cm. Gun, M. 95, in casemate (calibre 75 mm.). *Kasemattkanone*	M. 75 .... M. 75/85 c	Segment shell, M. 75. Shrapnel, M. 75/85 c.
8 cm. Gun, M. 94, in casemate (calibre 75 mm.). *Kasemattkanone*	M. 75	Segment shell, M. 75.
8 cm. old Field Gun. M. 75, fixed or movable armament (calibre 75 mm.).	M. 75 .... M. 85 .... —	Segment shell, M. 75. Shrapnel, M. 75/85. Case-shot.
8 cm. gun, M. 94, in cupola (calibre 75 mm.). *Panzerkanone*		
8 cm. Gun, M. 94 and 98, in casemate (calibre 75 mm.). *Minimalschartenkanone*	M. 75 .... M. 95	Segment shell, M. 94. Shrapnel, M. 96/95 and and 94/95.
8 cm. Fortress Gun, M. 94 on shielded carriage (calibre 75 mm.). *Panzerkanone*	—	Case-shot.
8 cm. captured Russian Field Gun (calibre mm.).	—	—

Piece.	Fuzes.	Projectiles.
8 cm. A.A. Gun, M. 14 L.Fa.Kan. (*Luftfahrzeug-abwehrkanone*)	—	—
9 cm. old Field Gun, M. 75 and 75/96 (calibre 87 mm.)	— M. 75	Segment shell, M. 75. Powder-filled steel shell M. 75.
9 cm. Gun in casemate, M. 75/4 and 11	91 *a* and *b* 96 .... 96 *a* and *c* —	Shrapnel, M. 75, 91 and 96. Case-shot.
10·4 cm. Light Field Howitzer, M. 99, 14 and 16 (calibre 104 mm.). *Leichte Feldhaubitze*)	M. 99, 10 cm. (with gaine)	Ammonal shell, M. 99, and 5.
10·4 cm. Howitzer in cupola, M. 99, 5, 6 and 9 (calibre 104 mm.) *Panzerhaubitze*)	M. 9, 10 cm. .... M. 99, 10 cm.	*Ekrasit* shell, M. 10/9 and 14/9. Shrapnel, M. 99.
10·4 cm. Mountain Howitzer, M. 99, 8, 10 and 16 (calibre 105 mm.). *Gebirgshaubitze*)	M. 99 *b* .... 10 cm., M. 14 .... E.H.Z. 17	Star-shell, M. 6/99 *b*. Universal shell. " Yellow cross " gas shell.
10·2 cm. Heavy Italian Gun	—	—
10·4 cm. Heavy Gun, M. 14, 15 and 12/16 (calibre 104 mm.)	10 cm., M. 14	Universal shell. Shrapnel. Shell steel, M. 14.
10·5 cm. Heavy German Gun, K. 04 (calibre 105 mm.)	Gr. Z. 94 H. Z. Vst. 14 .... Dopp. Z. 92	10 cm. Gr. 96. Shrapnel 96.
(?) 10·5 cm. Turkish Howitzer	—	—
12 cm. Heavy Gun, M. 80 (calibre 120 mm.)	M. 80 .... M. 6, 12 cm. (with gaine)	Powder-filled shell, M.80. *Ekrasit* shell, M. 80.
12 cm. Fortress Gun in turret, or casemate, M. 80 and 96 (calibre 120 mm.). *Minimal-schartenkanone*	M. 12 *b* (with gaine) M. 9 .... M. 12 *b* .... M. 93 *a* .... —	Steel shell, M. 12. Steel shell, M. 14/9. Shrapnel, M. 12. Shrapnel, M. 80/93 *a*. Case-shot.
12 cm. Gun, M. 61 and 61/95, Reserve of H.A. (calibre 120 mm.)	M. 61 .... M. 66 .... 66/85 K. 80 K. .... M. 1 and 1 *a*	Shrapnel, M. 61. Shrapnel, M. 66 and 78. Shell, M. 61.
13 cm. Heavy Gun, M. (?) (calibre mm)	—	—

Piece.	Fuzes.	Projectiles.
15 cm. Heavy Gun, M. 80 (calibre 149 mm.). *Belagerungskanone*	M. 80	Powder-filled shell, M. 80.
	M. 6, 15 cm. (with gaine)	Ekrasit shell, M. 80.
	M. 9	Ekrasit shell, M. 99/9.
	M. 9	Steel Shell, M. 15/9.
	M. 12 b (?)	Steel shell, M. 12.
	—	Shrapnel, M. 12.
	M. 93 a	Shrapnel, M. 80/93 a.
	—	Armour-piercing, M. 80.
15 cm. Coast Defence Gun, L/35 *Küstenkanone*	M. 80	Powder-filled shell, M. 80.
15 cm. Coast Defence Gun, L/40	M. 96	Shell, M. 97/95 and M. 98/96.
	15 cm., M. 8	Shell with false cap, M. 97/8 a and 98/8 a.
	M. 96 b	Shrapnel, M. 97/96 b.
	—	Armour-piercing, M. 97.
15 cm. Fortress Gun, M. 61 and 61/95, Reserve of H.A. (calibre 149 mm.)	M. 1 and 1 a	Shell, M. 61.
	M. 61	Shrapnel, M. 61.
	M. 66 .... ⎫	
	66/85 K. ⎬	Shrapnel, M. 66 and 76.
	80 K. .... ⎭	
15 cm. Long-range Russian Gun (calibre mm.)	—	—
14·9 cm. Heavy Italian Gun	—	—
14·9 cm. Heavy Italian Howitzer	—	—
15 cm. Heavy Field Howitzer, M. 94, 99, 94/4, 99/4, 14 (?) and 15 (calibre 149 mm.) *Batteriehaubitze, Schwere Feldhaubitze* or *Autohaubitze*	M. 80	Powder-filled shell, M. 80.
	M. 6, 15 cm.	Ekrasit shell, M. 80.
	M. 9, 15 cm.	Ekrasit shell, M. 99/9.
	M. 12 a	Steel shell, M. 12.
	M. 9	Steel shell, M. 15/9.
15 cm. Howitzer in cupola, M. 94 and 99 (calibre 149 mm.). *Panzerhaubitze*	M. 12 a	Steel shrapnel, M. 12.
	M. 93 a (with Ergänzungszünder)	Shrapnel, M. 80/93 a.
15 cm. Mortar, M. 80, 98, 98/7 and 16 (calibre 149 mm.). *Mörser in der Lafette*	M. 99 a	Star shell, M. 6/99 a.
	15 cm. M. 14	Universal shell, M. 14.
15 cm. Mortar, M. 80, in cupola (calibre, 149 mm.). — *Panzermörser* on *Mörser in der Schleife*	—	Gas shell.

Piece.	Fuzes.	Projectiles.
15 cm. Mortar, M. 78 (calibre 149·1 mm.).	M. 1 and 1 a	Powder-filled shell, M.16.
	M. 75	Powder-filled shell, M. 7.
	M. 93 a	Shrapnel, M. 78/93 a.
	M. 80 and 66/85 K.	Shrapnel, M. 66 and 78.
	M. 75 (with adapter)	Percussion-shrapnel, M. 66 and 78.
	M. 99 a	Star shell, M. 6/99 a.
15·2 cm. Heavy Gun, M.15 *Belagerungskanone*	Clockwork	Shrapnel.
18 cm. Short Gun, M. 80 (calibre 180 mm). *Belagerungskanone*	M. 80	Powder-filled shell, M. 80.
	M. 6, 18 cm.(with gaine)	*Ekrasit* shell, M. 80.
	M. 12	Steel shell, M. 12.
	M. 12	Steel shrapnel, M. 12.
	M. 93 a (*Ergänzungszünder*).	Shrapnel, M. 80/93 a.
21 cm. Mortar, M. 80 (Coast defence) and M. 16 (calibre mm.) *Küstenmörser* or *Mörser*.	M. 80	Powder-filled shell,M.80.
	M. 6, 21 cm.	*Ekrasitbombe*, M. 98.
	M. 99 a	Star shell, M. 99 a.
21 cm. Coast Defence Gun, L/20. *Küstenkanone*	M. 99	*Ekrasitbombe*, M. 99.
21 cm. Heavy Italian Howitzer	—	—
24 cm. Mortar, M. 98, 98/7, 95/10 and 10/5 (calibre 240 mm,). *Mörser*.	M. 9, 24 cm.	*Ekrasitbombe*, M. 98/9 and 6/9.
	M. 99 a	Star shell, M. 99 a.
24 cm. Gun, M. 16 (calibre mm.). *Belagerungskanone*	? M. 9, 24 cm..... Clockwork Dopp. Z. 16	? *Ekrastibombe*, M. 98/9 and 6/9.
24 cm. Coast Defence Gun L/22	24 cm. G. Z.	*Zündgranate*.
28 cm. Howitzer, M. (calibre mm.). *Belagerungshaubitze*	—	—

Piece.	Fuzes.	Projectiles.
28 cm. Coast Defence Gun, L/22 and L/35.	24 cm. G.Z. .... 28 cm. G.Z.	*Zündgranate.* *Zündgranate.*
30·5 cm. Mortar, M. 11 (calibre 305 mm.)	M. 9, 30·5 cm.	*Ekrasitbombe,* M. 11/9 and 15/9; *Truppenbombe.*
30·5 cm. Coast Defence Gun, L/40	30·5 cm., M. 8 .... M. 98/96	*Zündgranate.*
(?) 35 cm. Gun, M. 16 (B.K.L/45)	M. 9 (?)	H.E. Shell, M. 16.
38 cm. Naval Gun (calibre 381 mm.), L./40	—	H.E. Shell, M. 16.
38 cm. Howitzer, M. 16 (B.H.L/17)	—	H.E. Shell, M. 16.
42 cm. Howitzer, M. (?) (K.H.L/15)	—	H.E. Shell, M. 16.
(?) 42 cm. Mortar M. 15 (calibre mm.)	—	H.E. Shell, M. 16.

Page 11—

Insert the following list of " Abbreviations :—

LIST OF ABBREVIATIONS.

Abbreviation.	Signification.	English equivalent.
A.	Aufschlag	Percussion.
A.S.	Aufschlagszünder	Percussion fuze.
A.Z.	Aufschlagsschrapnell	Percussion shrapnel.
B.H.	Belagerungshaubitze	Siege howitzer.
B.K.	Belagerungskanone	Siege gun.
B.K.L/40	Belagerungskanone Länge 40 kaliber.	Siege gun, 40-calibre length.
B.Z.	Bodenzünder	Base percussion fuze.
D.Z.	Doppelzünder	Time and percussion fuze.
E.B.	Ekrasitbombo	Ecrasite shell, 21 cm. and over.
E.G.	Ekrasitgranate	Ecrasite shell.
E.H.Z.....	Empfindlicher Haubitz-zünder.	Instantaneous fuze for howitzers.
Ekr.	Ekrasit	Ecrasite.
E.K.Z.....	Empfindlicher Kanonen-zünder.	Instantaneous fuze for guns.
FeldHaub.	Feldhaubitze	Field howitzer.
FeldKan.	Feldkanone	Field gun.
G. or **Gr.**	Granate	Shell.
G.Z. or **Gr.Z.**	Granatenzünder	Percussion fuze.
Haub.	Haubitze	Howitzer.
K.	Kartätschschrapnell (or Kornpulver).	Case-shot effect (or *Kornpulver* time-composition).
Kan.	Kanone	Gun.
K.H.L/15	Küstenhaubitze Länge 15	Coast Defence Howitzer, 15-calibre length.
K.L.fa.Kan.	Kraftwagenluftfahrzeug-abwehrkanone.	A.A. gun on lorry.
L.fa.Kan.	Luftfahrzeugabwehr-kanone.	A.A. gun.
L.S.	Leuchtschrapnell....	Star shell.
M.	Muster	Pattern.
Mörs. or **Mrs.**	Mörser	Mortar.
n/A.	neue Art	New model.
S. or **Schr.**	Schrapnell....	Shrapnel.
S.D.Z.	Schrapnelldoppelzünder	Time and percussion fuze.
V.	Vortempierung	" Anticipated burst " (see pp. 64 *et seq.*)
Z.	Zünder	Fuze.
Z.V.	Zündvorrichtung....	Base percussion fuze.
Z.V.V.	Zünderverzögerungs-vorrichtung.	Delay action.

Page 12—

1875 Pattern Percussion Fuze.

After line 15, *add*—

21 cm. Coast Defence Mortar, M. 73 ; maximum range, 5,000 metres.

Page 14—

1880 Pattern Percussion Fuze.

Line 12.—*After* " 15 cm. Coast Defence Gun, L/35," *add*—

Maximum range, 9,000 metres.

Page 18—

1906 Pattern Percussion Fuze.

Line 17.—*After* " 21 cm. Coast Defence Mortar " *insert* " 1873 " ; and *add*—

Maximum range of 1880 model, 7,200 metres.

Page 28—

1909 Pattern Base Percussion Fuze.

After line 9, *insert* :—

" 21 cm. Coast Defence Mortar, M. 73. Max. range, 5,000 metres.

(?) 21 cm. Mortar, M. 16."

Line 11.—*For* " 6,500 metres " *read* " 7,200 metres."

Page 30—

30·5 cm. Base Percussion Fuze.

Line 3.—*For* " 12,800 metres " *read* " 9,500 metres."

After line 9, insert :—

" This fuze is possibly identical with the 30·5 cm. *Zünd-vorrichtung* (Z.V., M.8) used with 30·5 cm. Coast Defence Gun L/40 ; range, 18,000 metres.

On the blank pages following page 34, insert :—

1896 Pattern Percussion Fuze.

Designation.—G.Z. M. 96.

Used with,—15 cm. Coast Defence Gun L/40 (max. range, 10,000 metres) with shells, M. 97/95 and 98/96.

Graduations.—None.

Material.—Brass.

Remarks.—
Shell M. 97/8a, with false cap and Base-percussion fuze 15 cm.
Z.V., M. 8, is also used ; as well as shell M. 98/8a.

1897 Pattern Percussion Fuze.

Designation.—G.Z. M. 97.

Used with.—7 cm. Coast Defence Gun, L/42 (max. range, 6,000 metres), with shell M. 98.

Graduations.—None.

Material.—Brass.

Remarks.—

1898 Pattern Percussion Fuze.

Designation.—G.Z. M. 98.

Used with.—
6 cm. Gun in casemate, M. 98 and 9.
6 cm. Gun in movable turret, M 98, with 1898 pattern shell.
Max. range, 1,500 metres.

Graduations.—Nil.

Material.—Brass.

Remarks.—

1899 Pattern Percussion Fuze.

Designation.—G.Z. M. 99.

Used with.—21 cm. Coast Defence Mortar, M. 80, with steel " Bombe," M. 80 ; max. range, 7,200 metres.

Graduations.—Nil.

Material.—

Remarks.

24 cm. Percussion Fuze.

Designation.—G.Z. 24 c.m.

Used with.—
21 cm. Coast Defence Gun, L/20 ; range, 4,000 metres.
24 cm. Coast Defence Gun, L/22 ; range, 6,000 metres.
28 cm. Coast Defence Gun, L/22 ; range, 13,500 metres.

Graduations.—Nil.

Material.—

Remarks.—

28 cm. Percussion Fuze.

Designation.—28 cm. G.Z.

Used with.—28 cm. Coast Defence Gun, L/35 and L/35a and b ; max. range, 13,500 metres.

Graduations.—Nil.

Material.

Remarks.—

1916 Pattern German Instantaneous Gun Fuze.

Designation.—E.K.Z. 16 (*Empfindlicher Kanonenzünder*).

Used with.—8 cm. Field Gun M. 5 and 5/8 with " Blue Cross " gas shell ("sneezing gas ") ; range, 8,300 metres.

Graduations.—

Material—

Remarks.—
See " Notes on German Fuzes." (2nd Edition.)

1917 Pattern German Instantaneous Gun Fuze.

Designation.—E.K.Z. 17 (*Empfindlicher Kanonenzünder*).

Used with.—8 cm. Field Gun M. 5 and 5/8 with " Yellow Cross " gas shell (" mustard gas ") ; range, 8,300 metres.

Graduations.—None.

Material.

Remarks.—
See " Notes on German Fuzes." (2nd Edition.)

1917 Pattern German Instantaneous Howitzer Fuze.

Designation.—E.H.Z. 17 (*Empfindlicher Haubitzzünder*).

Used with.—

10.4 cm. Light Field Howitzer, M. 99, 14 and 16.
10.4 cm. Mountain Howitzer, M. 99, 8, 10 and 16 with " Yellow Cross " (" mustard gas ") shell.
Range, 8,800 metres.

Graduations.—

Material.—

Remarks.—
See " Notes on German Fuzes."

Page 50—

1875 Pattern Time Fuze.

Line 2.—*For* " 1894 " *read* " 1895."

Line 3.—*For* " 2,500 metres " *read* " 3,000 metres."

Page 52—

1880 Pattern Time Fuze.

Lines 4 and 5.—*After* " 12 cm. and 15 cm. Guns (1861 and 61/95) " *insert* :

" Max. range, 4,000 metres."

Line 7.—*After* " 15 cm. Mortar (1878) " *insert* :
" Max. range, 2,800 metres."

Page 56—

1891 Pattern Time and Percussion Fuze.

Lines 4 and 6.—*For* " 3,375 metres " *read* " 4,800 metres."

Page 58—

1893 Pattern Time and Percussion Fuze.

Line 8.—*After* " 15 cm. Howitzer in cupola " *insert* :
" Max. range, 5,800 metres."

Line 11 : *For* " 3,200 metres " *read* " 2,800 metres."

Table at bottom of page 3, column 3.—*For* " 5,900 metres " *read*
" 5,800 metres."

Page 62—

1895 Pattern Time and Percussion Fuze.

Remarks.—*Insert*: T. and P. fuze M. 95*a* is used with shrapnel M. 98 for 7 cm. Coast Defence Gun L/42 ; range, 3,500 metres.

Page 66—

1896 Pattern Time and Percussion Fuze.

Line 1.—**Designation.**—*After* " 96*a* " *insert* " 96*b*."

Line 14.—**Remarks.**—*Add* " M. 96*b* is used with Shrapnel, M.97/ 96*b* for 15 cm. Coast Defence Gun, L/40 ; range, 6,000 metres.

On one of the blank pages at end of book insert :—

Clockwork Time Fuze.

Designation.—

Used with.—

8 cm. Field Gun, M. 5 and 5/8, with long H.E. shell, M. 14 (?)

15.2 cm. Heavy Gun, M. 15 ; with shrapnel, range about 20,000 metres.

(?) 24 cm. Siege Gun, M. 16.

Graduations.—

Material.—Body, brass ; cap, housing, steel ; housing for percussion system, aluminium.

Remarks.—

The clockwork fuzes which are being tried in the Austro-Hungarian army are probably of German manufacture (See " Notes on German Fuzes," 1918 edition, and " Reports on Enemy Ammunition," No. 20 (September, 1917), published by the Ministry of Munitions.

15.2 cm. guns identified on the Italian front at Cà Vecchia (Monte Cimone) have shelled Thiene at a range of 17 km. and Villaverla (about 20 km.), with shrapnel fuzed with a clockwork fuze.

NOTES

ON

AUSTRO-HUNGARIAN FUZES.

NOVEMBER, 1917.

Prepared by the General Staff

Naval & Military Press Ltd

CONTENTS.

	Page
Preface	3
List of Austro-Hungarian Artillery Fuzes	4
Table showing Fuzes and Projectiles used with various Guns, Howitzers and Mortars	5
Marks on Austrian Fuzes	7
Note on the Metals used	8
Austro-Hungarian Artillery terms	9
Percussion Fuzes	12
Time Fuzes	46
Time and Percussion Fuzes	56
Conversion Tables	Covers.

Some pages are numbered but blank as per the original, this was to allow the pasting of amendments.

(B 11931) Wt. w. 4412—PP694 2250 2/18 H & S P. 17/939

PREFACE.

THESE " Notes " have been put together from data provided by the Italian and Russian General Staffs, and from other sources. The *Dati e cenni su materiali dell' Artiglieria Austro-Ungarica*, by Colonel Forni, has been of great value ; and thanks are due to the Italian General Staff for permission to reproduce the illustrations from this book. The details given here are necessarily incomplete ; the information on certain points is conflicting and possibly inaccurate It is hoped that General Staff Officers, and all Artillery Officers with their batteries will do their utmost to obtain additional information on the subject of Austro-Hungarian fuzes and forward it to G.H.Q. for transmission to the War Office, so that the book may be kept up to date.

Fuzes are an invaluable guide to what batteries the enemy has against us in any particular sector ; and any evidence as to the nature and calibre of the guns with which each fuze is employed, will be particularly useful.

M.I. 3 (b),
November, 1917.

CLASSIFIED INDEX OF AUSTRO-HUNGARIAN FUZES.

				Page
Percussion	Nose-percussion	External	M. 75 (Fig. 1)	12
			M. 80 (Fig. 2)	14
			M. 1 (Fig. 3)	16
			M. 1 a	16
			M. 6 (Fig. 4)	18
			Gr.Z. 04 (Fig. 5)	20
			H.Z. 14 (Fig. 6)	22
		Internal	10·5 cm. (Fig. 7)	24
	Base-percussion....		M. 98 (Fig. 8)	25
			M. 9 (Fig. 9)	28
			30·5 cm. (Fig. 10)	30
			30·5 cm. (Fig. 11)	32
			38 cm.	34
			42 cm.	36
Time	Un-Graduated		M. 61	46
			M. 66	48
			M. 66/85 K. (Fig. 12)	48
			M. 80 K. (Fig. 14)	52
	Graduated		M. 75/85 c. (Fig. 13)	50
			M. 85	54
Time and Percussion	One Time Ring	Marked "A"	M. 91 a	56
			M. 91 b	56
			M. 93 a (Fig. 15)	58
			Ergänzungszünder (Fig. 16)	60
			M. 95 (Fig. 17)....	62
		Marked "A" and "V," M. 95 b	64
		Marked "A," "V" and "K"	M. 96	66
			M. 96 a (Fig. 18)	66
			M. 96 c	66
			M. 99, 7 cm. (Fig. 19)....	68
			M. 99, 10 cm. (Fig. 20)	70
			M. 99 a (Fig. 21)	74
			M 99 b	76
			M. 2	78
			M. 5 (Fig. 22)	80
			M. 8 bronze (Fig. 23)	82
			M. 8 bronze (Fig. 24)	84
			M. 8 iron (Fig. 25)	86
			M. 12 (Fig. 27)....	90
			M. 12 a (Fig. 28)	92
			M. 12 b (Fig. 29)	94
			M. 12 f (Fig. 30)	96
			Schrapnellgranate fuze (Fig. 31)	98
			German fuze, Dopp.-Z. 92, 10 cm. K. (Fig. 32)	100
	Two time-rings, M. 8 B Zusatzladung (Fig. 26)			88

5

FUZES AND PROJECTILES USED WITH VARIOUS GUNS, HOWITZERS AND MORTARS.

Piece.	Fuzes.	Projectiles.
3·7 Trench Gun (calibre 37 mm.)	—	*Minengranate Brisantsgranate* Star-shell.
6 cm. Gun, M. 98, in casemate mounting, or movable turret (calibre 57 mm.)	M. 98 .... M. 95b	Powder-filled shell, M.98. Shrapnel, M. 98/95, Case shot.
6 cm. Gun, M. 99, in casemate	M. 98	Powder-filled shell, M.98.
7 cm. Mountain Gun, M. 99, 8 and 9 (calibre 72.5 mm.)	M. 99, 7 cm. (with gaine) M. 99, 7 cm.	*Ekrasit* shell, M. 99 and 5. Shrapnel, M. 99.
7.5 cm. Mountain Gun, M. 15	7 cm., M. 15	*Schrapnellgranate* (universal shell).
8 cm. Field Gun, M. 5 and 5/8 (calibre 76.5 mm.) 8 cm. Fortress Gun, M.5 and 5/9	M. 5, 8 and 8 b (with gaines) M. 5, 8 and 8 b....	*Ammonal* shell, M. 5 and 8. Shrapnel, M. 5 and 8.
8 cm. Gun, in turret, M. 2	M. 2 .... —	Shrapnel, M. 2. Case-shot.
8 cm. Gun, M. 95, in casemate (old field gun, '75 pattern) (calibre 75 mm.)	M. 75 .... M. 75/85 c	Segment shell, M. 75. Shrapnel, M. 75/85c.
8 cm. Gun, M. 94, in casemate (old field gun)	M. 75	Segment shell, M. 75.
8 cm. old Field Gun, M. 75 (fixed or movable armament)	M. 75 .... M. 85 .... —	Segment shell, M. 75. Shrapnel, M. 75/85. Case shot.
8 cm. Gun, M. 94, in cupola 8 cm. Guns, M. 94 and 98, in casemate mountings 8 cm. Fortress Gun, M. 94, on shielded carriage	M. 75 .... M. 95 .... —	Segment shell, M. 94. Shrapnel, M. 96/95 and 94/95. Case shot.
9 cm. old Field Guns, M. 75 and 75/96 (calibre 87 mm.) 9 cm. Gun, M. 75/4, and 11 in casemate mounting	M. 75 .... M. 91 a, 91 b, 96, 96 a, 96 c —	Segment shell, M. 75. Powder-filled shell, M. 75. Shrapnel, M. 75. 91 and 96. Case shot.
10 cm. Light Field Howitzer, M. 99 and 14 (calibre 104 mm.) **10 cm. Mountain Howitzer, M. 99, 8, 10 and 16** 10 cm. Howitzer, in cupola, M. 99, 5, 6 and 9	M. 99, 10 cm. (with gaine) M. 9 .... M. 99, 10 cm. .... M. 99b .... 10 cm., M. 14	*Ammonal* shell, M. 99 and 5. *Ekrasit* shell, M. 10/9 and 14. Shrapnel, M. 99. Star-shell, M. 6/99b. Universal shell.

Note.—The more important guns are printed in **heavy type.**

Piece.	Fuzes.	Projectiles.
10.4 cm. Heavy Gun, M. 14, 15 and 12/15 (calibre 104 mm.)	10 cm., M. 14 .... / ? / ?	Universal shell. / Shrapnel. / Steel shell.
10 cm. Heavy German Gun, K. 04 (calibre 105 mm.)	Gr.Z. 04.... .... / H.Z. Vst. 14 .... / Dopp.Z. 92	10 cm., Gr. 96. / 10 cm., Gr. 96. / Shrapnel 96.
12 cm. Heavy Gun, M. 80 (calibre 120 mm.) 12 cm. Fortress Gun, M. 80 and 96, in casemate or turret	M. 80 .... / M. 6, 12 cm. .... / M. 9 .... / M. 93 a .... / M. 12 b	Powder-filled shell, M.80. / Ekrasit shell, M. 80. / Steel shell, M. 14/9. / Shrapnel, M. 80/93 a. / New steel shell, and shrapnel, M. 12 / Case-shot.
12 cm. Gun, M. 61 and 61/95 (mobile reserve of H.A.)	M. 61 .... / M. 66, 66/85 K., 80 K. / M. 1 and 1 a .... / —	Shrapnel, M. 61. / Shrapnel, M. 66 and 78. / Powder filled shell, M.61. / Case-shot.
15 cm. Heavy Gun, M. 80 (calibre 149 mm.)	M. 80 .... / M. 6, 15 cm. .... / M. 9 .... / M. 12 b .... / M. 93 a .... / —	Powder-filled shell, M.80. / Ekrasit shell, M. 80. / Ekrasit shell, M. 99/9. / Steel shell and shrapnel, M. 12. / Shrapnel, M. 80/93 a. / Armour-piercing shell, M. 80.
15 cm. Coast Defence Gun 15 cm. Fortress Gun, M. 61 and 61/95 (reserve of H.A.)	M. 80 .... / M. 61 .... / M. 66, 66/85 K. and 80 K. / M. 1 and 1 a	Shell / Shrapnel, M. 61. / Shrapnel, M. 66 and 78. / Powder-filled shell, M.6.
15 cm. Mortar, M. 78 (mobile Reserve)	M. 75 .... / M. 75 (with adapter) / M. 80 and 66/85 K. / M. 93a .... / M. 93 a (with Ergänzungszünder) / M. 99 a	Powder-filled shell, M.78. / Percussion-shrapnel, M. 66 and 78. / Shrapnel, M. 66 and 78. / Shrapnel, M. 78/93 a. / Shrapnel, M. 80/93 a. / Star-shell, M. 6/99 a.
15 cm. Heavy Field Howitzer, M. 94, 99, 94/4 99/4 and 15 (calibre 149 mm.) 15 cm. howitzer in cupola, M. 94 and 99 **15 cm. Mortar, M. 80, 98, 98/7 and 16**	M. 80 .... / M. 6, 15 cm. .... / M. 9, 15 cm. .... / — / M. 12 a .... / M. 93 a (with Ergänzungszünder) / M. 99 a	Powder-filled shell,M.80. / Ekrasit shell, M. 80. / Ekrasit shell, M. 99/9. / Steel shell M. 15/9. / Steel shell and shrapnel, M. 12. / Shrapnel, M. 80/83 a. / Star-shell, M. 6/99 a.
15 cm. Mortar, M. 80, in cupola or on sledge	15 cm. M. 14 .... / ?	Universal shell, M. 14. / Gas shell.

Piece.	Fuzes.	Projectiles.
18 cm. Heavy Gun, M. 80 (calibre 180 mm.)	M. 80	Powder-filled shell,M.80.
	M. 12 (?)	Steel shell and shrapnel, M. 12.
	M. 6, 18 cm.	*Ekrasit* shell.
	M. 93 a)with *Ergänzungszünder*)	Shrapnel, M. 80/93 a.
21 cm. Coast Defence Gun, L./20	M. 6 (?), 21 cm.	*Ekrasit* shell, M. 99.
21 cm. Coast Defence Mortar, M. 80. and Mortar, M. 15	M. 6, 21 cm.	*Ekrasit* shell, M. 99.
	M. 99 a	Star-shell, M. 99 a.
24 cm. Mortar, M. 98, 98/7, 15/10, and 10/15 (calibre 240 mm.)	M. 9, 24 cm.	*Ekrasitbombe*, M. 98/9 and 6/9
24 cm Gun, M. 16	M. 99 a	Star-shell, M. 99 a.
28 cm. Howitzer or Mortar		
30·5 cm. Mortar.	M. 9, 30·5 cm.	*Ekrasitbombe* M. 11/9
35 cm. Gun, M. 16.		and 15/9 ; *Truppenbombe.*
38 cm. Naval Gun.		
42 cm. Mortar.		
42 cm. Howitzer,		

MARKS ON AUSTRIAN FUZES.

Nearly every Austrian fuze bears a mark showing the **Year** in which it was adopted. This mark consists of the letter " M." (*Muster*, Pattern) followed by a numeral denoting the year. Thus the 1908 pattern time and percussion fuze, employed with 8 cm. field artillery shells, is marked *M.* 8.

A **Small Letter** sometimes follows the numeral ; but the same letters do not always mean the same thing. The 1893 pattern T. and P. fuze, for instance, is always marked *M.* 93a. The extrafuze (*Ergänzungszünder*), sometimes screwed over the cap to increase the range at which time-shrapnel can be fired with it, is marked *M.* 93a if intended for guns (12 cm. or 15 cm.) ; or *M.* 93b, if intended for Howitzers (15 cm.). On the contrary, the 1912 pattern T. and P. fuze is marked *M.* 12a when employed with Howitzers or Mortars (15 cm.) ; but *M.* 12b when employed with guns (12 cm. or 15 cm.). Again, the T. and P. fuze of 1899 pattern, used with star-shells, is marked *M.* 99a when adapted for shells of 15 cm. calibre or over ; *M.* 99b if it is for shells of 10 cm. calibre.

Some fuzes are marked with the **Calibre** of the gun, as well as the date, e.g., the 1906 pattern percussion fuze, used with high explosive (*Ekrasit*) shells, is marked 12 *cm.* M. 6 or 21 *cm.* M. 6, according to the size of shell to which it may be fitted. The T. and P. fuzes belonging to Mountain Artillery are also marked in this way; e.g., *M*. 99, 7 *cm*. for 7 cm. Mountain Gun, *M*. 99, 10 *cm*. for 10 cm. Light Field Howitzer or 10 cm. Mountain Howitzer.

Graduations on the time-rings of T. and P. fuzes are described under each fuze. In the newer patterns they are all in *hundreds of metres*; but older fuzes have been employed against the Italian front, e.g., *M*. 91 *a*, *M*. 91 *b*, in which the time-ring was graduated in *hundreds of paces*. In the 1899-pattern fuze for star-shells (*M*. 99 *a* and *M*. 99*b*) the graduation is in hundreths of the length of the time-composition. No Austrian fuze appears to be graduated in seconds.

The letters **A**, **V** and **K** are engraved on the time-rings of most T. and P. fuzes. Of these "A" indicates the setting for *Aufschlag*, "percussion"; "V," *Vortempierung*, an "anticipated burst," from 200 to 400 metres from the muzzle; "K," *Kartätschschrapnell*, a burst with case-shot effect.

In certain time fuzes of very old design, M. 66/85 K and M. 80 K, which are said to have been used in this campaign with the reserve of heavy artillery (particularly in mountain defence), the letter **K** signified the quality of powder in the time-composition, *Kornpulver*.

Before the combined Austro-German offensive in Italy in the Autumn of 1917, only three German fuzes were used by the Austrians, with 10·5 cm. guns of German make. These fuzes have special markings, and are described separately.

NOTE ON THE METALS USED.

The raw material used for fuzes in the Austro-Hungarian Artillery does not appear to have undergone much change since the beginning of the war. The metal is of good quality, and the workmanship generally proves to be accurate.

A tendency to contain less bronze and brass has been observed in various fittings connected with other artillery material. These metals are being replaced, in varying degrees, by steel and iron; and by a hard, white metal composed of an alloy of zinc with small proportions of copper, lead and iron. Copper, too, is being replaced by this alloy; and layers or bands of lead have been noted in parts subject to pressure.

These changes have been noticed also in projectiles of medium calibre, dating from 1915; but they have not yet led to the complete disuse of bronze and brass in fittings or driving bands. As a general rule, the driving band of an Austrian shell is of copper, excellently cut, and without flaws, which proves that the metal is uniform and compact in texture, and that the rifling of the gun is in good order.

Not much information is available as to bronze or brass in fuzes being replaced by other metals; it will be seen, however, that the 1908 pattern time and percussion fuze is now being made of iron with brass time-ring (page 86); while the *Zusatzladung* T. and P. fuze M. 8 b, with two graduated brass rings for use with different charges (*see* page 88), is made of a leaden-coloured alloy, covered with varnish to look like brass or to preserve it from oxidation. This fuze is one of the latest to be adopted by the Austro-Hungarian Artillery; it was not employed against the Italians until 1916.

It cannot be too strongly urged that any new facts which may be brought to light, bearing on the material and construction of enemy fuzes, should be reported as early as possible to G.H.Q.

TERMS COMMONLY USED WITH AUSTRO-HUNGARIAN FUZES.

Aufschlag.—Percussion (abbrev. " A " on time-ring).

Aufschlagszünder.—Percussion fuze.

Bodenzünder.—Base percussion fuze.

Doppelzünder.—Time and percussion fuze.

Ekrasit.—High explosive.

Ekrasitbombe.—H.E. shell used with 24-cm. mortar.

Ekrasitgranate.—Generally used for H.E. shell of all calibres, except 24 cm.

Ergänzungszünder.—A " supplementary fuze," screwed over the head of another to increase the range over which time-shrapnel may be fired with it.

Feldhaubitze.—" Field Howitzer " ; the light field howitzer (*leichte Feldhaubitze*) is of 10-cm. calibre ; the heavy field howitzer (*Schwere Feldhaubitze*), 15 cm.

Feldkanone.—" Field Gun " (8 cm.).

Granate.—" Shell."

Haubitze.—" Howitzer."

Kanone.—" Gun."

Kartätschschrapnell.—" Case-shot." " K " on time-ring of T. and P. fuze indicates setting at which case-shot effect may be obtained.

Kornpulver.—A special powder used in the time-composition of certain old-fashioned time fuzes. Also abbreviated " K."

Leichttempierbar.—" Easily set " ; used of a T. and P. fuzer which may be set by hand.

Leuchtschrapnell.—Star-shell (or *Leuchtgranate*).

Mörser.—Mortar (abbreviation, *Mrs.*).

Muster.— Pattern (abbrev. M).

Panzerhaubitze.—Howitzer in cupola, or with overhead shield.

Portee.—Range.

Schrapnelldoppelzünder.—T. and P. fuze for shrapnel.

Schrapnellgranate.—Universal shell.

Umgearbeitet.—" Modified."

Verzögerung.—Delay action (only in German-made fuzes).

Vorstecker.—" Safety-pin " (abbreviation, Vst., Vrst., or Vorst., in German fuzes).

Vortempierung.—Setting fuze for " anticipated burst," 200—400 metres from muzzle.

Zinnkupfer.—An alloy of tin and copper, containing a small proportion of tin.

Zünder.—Fuze.

Zünderverzögerungsvorrichtung.—Arrangement for delay action.

Zusatzladung.—" Additional charge " (*see* page 88).

11

1875 Pattern Percussion Fuze.

Designation.—M. 75.

Used with.—

8 cm. (old) Field Gun, M. 75, fixed or movable armament.
8 cm. fortress Gun, M. 94 and 95, in casemate.
(Max. range with 1875 pattern shell, 3,375 metres.)
8 cm. Gun, M. 94, in cupola.
8 cm. Gun, M. 94 and 98 in casemate.
8 cm. Gun, M. 94, on shielded carriage.
(Max. range with 1894 pattern shell, 4,000 metres.)
9 cm. (old) Field Gun, M. 75 and 75/96.
9 cm. Gun, M. 75/4, in casemate.
(Max. range with 1875 pattern shell, 6,450 metres.)
15 cm. Mortar, M. 78 (mobile reserve).
(Max. range with 1878 shell, 3,600 metres. With per-
cussion-shrapnel and adapter, Max. range, 3,200 metres.)

Graduations.—None.

Material.—Brass.

Remarks.—

1875 Pattern Percussion Fuze.

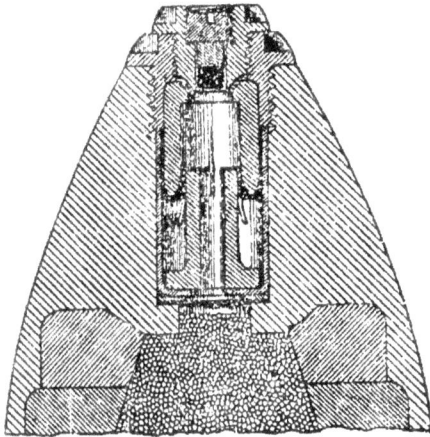

FIG. 1.

Percussion fuze M. 75 in powder-filled shell of 9 cm. gun (fixed armament).

1880 Pattern Percussion Fuze.

Designation.—M. 80.

Used with 1880 powder-filled and *Ekrasit* shell, for—

12 cm. Heavy Gun, 1880 ; max. range, 8,000 metres.
12 cm. Gun, 1880 and '96 (fixed armament).
15 cm. Heavy Gun, 1880 ; max. range, 8,500 metres.
15 cm. Heavy Field Howitzer, 1894, '99, 1915 ; max. range, 6,200 metres.
15 cm. Fortress Howitzer in cupola, 1894, and '99.
15 cm. Mortar, 1880, '98, '98/7 and 16 ; max. range, 3,500 metres.
15 cm. Mortar, 1880 (fixed armament) ; max. range, 3,500 metres.
15 cm. Coast Defence Gun, L/35.
18 cm. Heavy Gun, 1880 ; with 1880 shell ; max. range, 5,100 metres.
21 cm. Coast Defence Mortar, 1880, and Mortar, 1916.

Graduations.—None.

Material.—Brass.

Remarks.—Fuzes intended for 12 cm. shell are marked " 8 L," and are closed by a plain zinc plug.

Fuzes for 15 cm. and 18 cm. shell are marked " 4 L " ; the plug has a detent spring.

1880 Pattern Percussion Fuze.

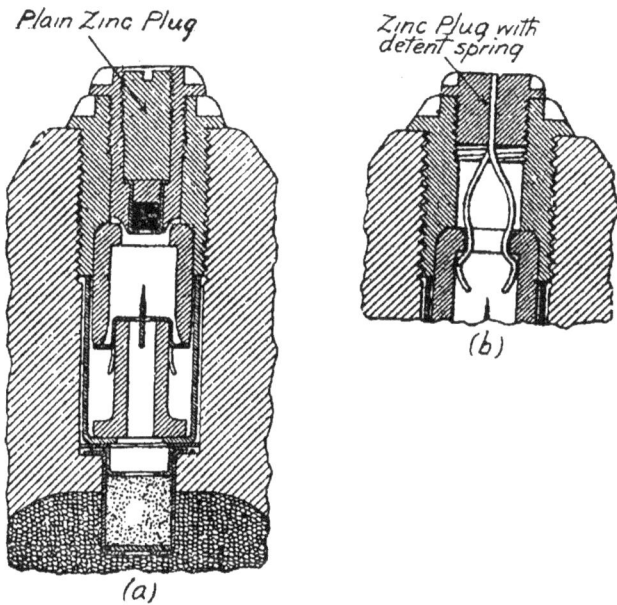

FIG. 2.

Percussion fuze M. 80.—(*a*) In 12 cm. common shell; (*b*) in 15 cm. or 18 cm. shell.

1901 Pattern Percussion Fuze.

Designation.—M. 1 and M. 1a.

Used with—

12 cm. Gun, 1861 and '61/95 (mobile reserve of heavy artillery); with 1861 shell; max. range 2,300 metres.

15 cm. Gun, 1861 and '61/95 (mobile reserve) with 1861 shell; max. range, 5,800 metres.

Graduations.—None.

Material.—Brass.

Remarks.—

Reported to have been used by the Austrians in Val Camonica and Val Giudicaria. The shells are of cast iron with a jacket of lead, and propelled by black powder. They are no longer used.

1901 Pattern Percussion Fuze.

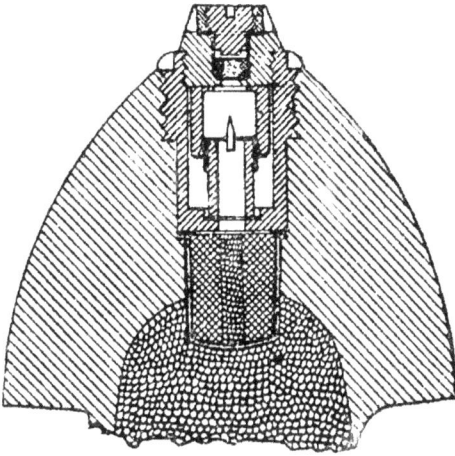

Fig. 3.

Percussion fuze M. 1 in 1861 shell used with 12 cm. or 15 cm. guns ('61 and 61/95 models) of mobile reserve.

6 Pattern Percussion Fuze.

Designation.—M. 6.

Used with—

Ekrasitgranate, 1880 pattern.

12 cm. Heavy Gun, 1880 ; max. range with *Ekrasit* shell, 8,000 metres.

12 cm. Gun, fixed armament, M. 80 and 96.

15 cm. Heavy Gun, 1880; max. range, 8,500 metres.

15 cm. Heavy Field Howitzer, 1894, '99 and 1915 ; max. range, 6,200 metres.

15 cm. Fortress Howitzer (*Panzerhaubitze*) 1894 and '99 ; max. range, 6,200 metres.

15 cm. Mortar, 1880, '98, '98/7 and 1916 ; max. range, 3,500 metres.

15 cm. Mortar, 1880 (in cupola) ; max. range, 3,500 metres.

18 cm. Heavy Gun, 1880 ; max. range, 5,100 metres.

21 cm. Coast Defence Gun, L/20.

21 cm. Coast Defence Mortar, 1880, and Mortar, 1916.

Graduations.—None.

Material.—Brass.

Remarks.—These fuzes are like the 1880 pattern percussion fuzes ; but have e   'al case, containing a gaine, screwed to the base. They are a.   .rked with the calibre, as well as the year of manufacture ; e.g., " 12 cm. M. 6," " 21 cm. M. 6."

1906 Pattern Percussion Fuze.

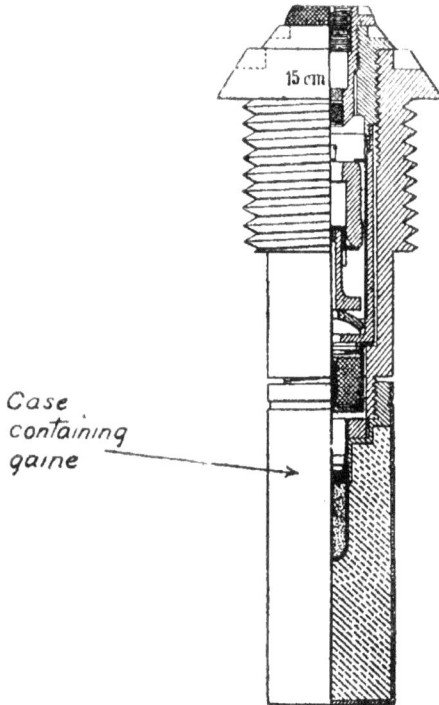

15 cm

Case
containing
gaine

FIG. 4.

Percussion fuze (1906) fitted with gaine, for *Ekrasit* shells, 12 cm.,
15 cm. and 18 cm. guns ; 15 cm. how. ; 15 cm. and 21 cm. mortar.

1904 Pattern Percussion Fuze (German make).

Designation.—Gr. Z. 04, i.e., *Granat-Zünder*, 1904.

Used with.—10·5 cm. German Gun ; 1896 pattern shell ; range, 10,300 metres.

Graduations.—None.

Material.—Brass and steel, with steel gaine.

Remarks.—Percussion ; with or without delay action.

"M.V." (*mit Verzögerung*), with delay.
"O.V." (*ohne Verzögerung*) without.

This fuze is extensively used for gas shells.

1904 Pattern Percussion Fuze (German make).

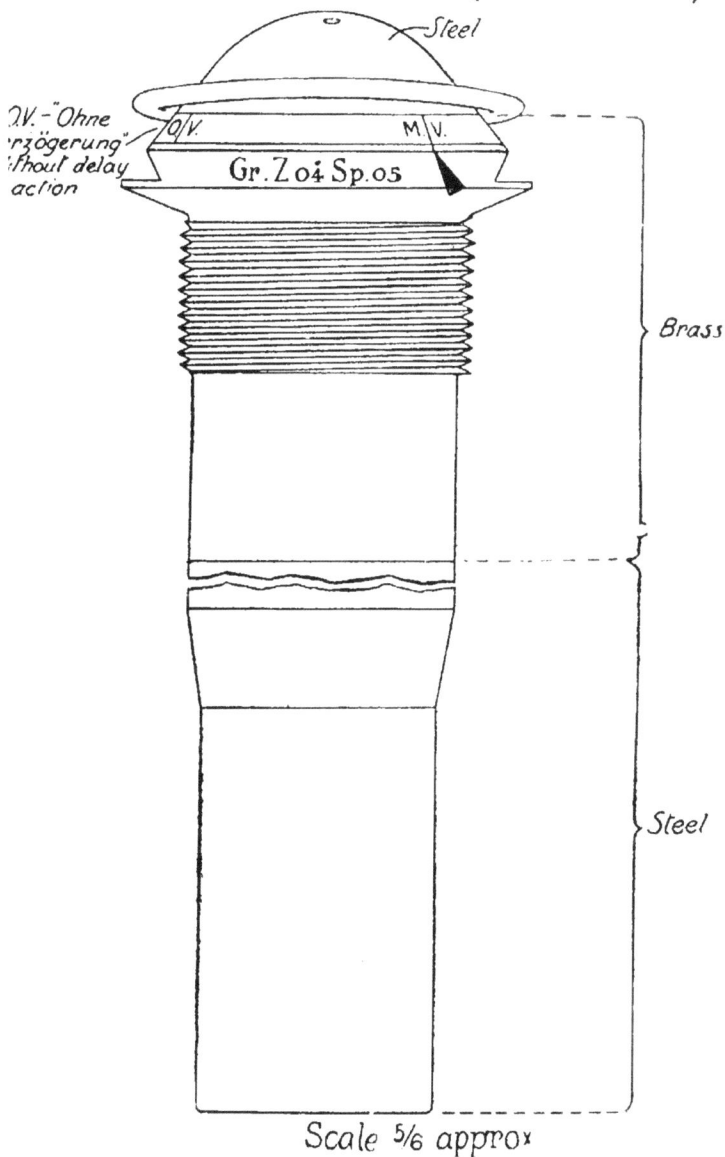

Steel

O.V.-"Ohne
Verzögerung"
without delay
action

O/V.   M.V.

Gr. Z o4 Sp. o5

Brass

Steel

Scale ⅚ approx

FIG. 5.—German percussion fuze Gr. Z. 04 used with 110·5 cm.
gun of German manufacture, often with gas shells.

1914 Pattern Percussion Fuze (German make).

Designation.—H. Z. 14 Vst., *i.e.*, *Haubitz-Zünder* 1914, *mit Vorstecker* (Howitzer-Fuze with safety-pin).

Used with.—10·5 cm. German Gun : 1914 and '14a pattern shell. Range, 10,300 metres.

Graduations.—None.

Material.—Brass, or brass with steel head.

Remarks.—The Italian authorities state that H. Z. 14 fuze has been used against them, in 1896 pattern shell from 10.5 cm. German gun. On the Western front this fuze is only employed in 1914-15 shell, with 10-cm. light field howitzer. But as they describe a fuze with safety-pin, it is probably H.Z. 14 Vst., which is known to be used with 10.5 cm. gun.

Vorstecker (safety-pin) is sometimes abbreviated *Vorst.* or *Vrst.* as well as *Vst.*

O or * stamped on head of fuze means that it is of superior quality.

1914 Pattern Percussion Fuze
(German make).

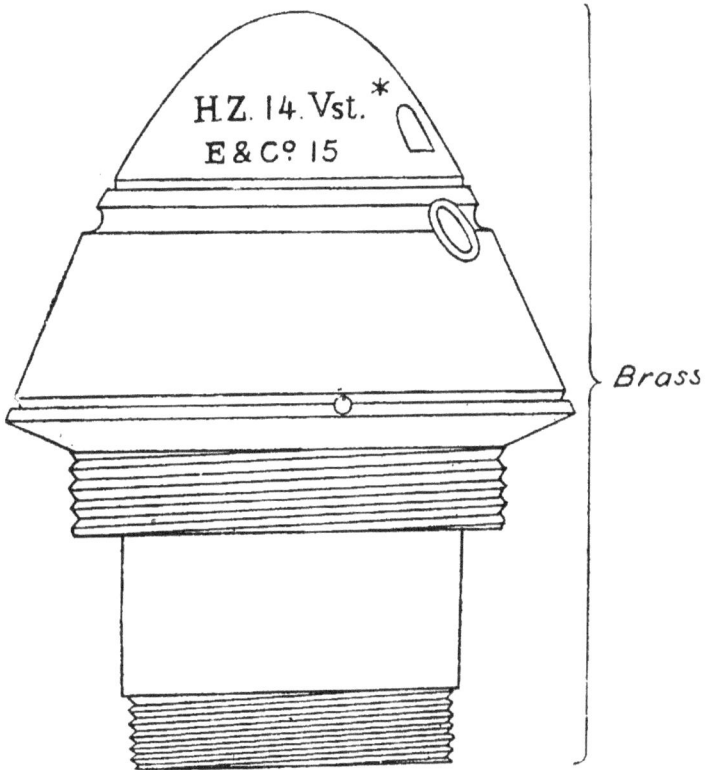

Full size.

FIG. 6.

German percussion fuze H. Z. 14 Vst. used with 10·4 cm. gun
of German manufacture.

Internal Nose Percussion Fuze for 10·4 cm. Shell.

Designation.—

10 cm. M. 14.

Used with—10.5 cm. heavy gun ; max. range, 12,500 metres.

Graduations.—None.

Material.—

Internal Nose Percussion Fuze for 10·5 cm Shell.

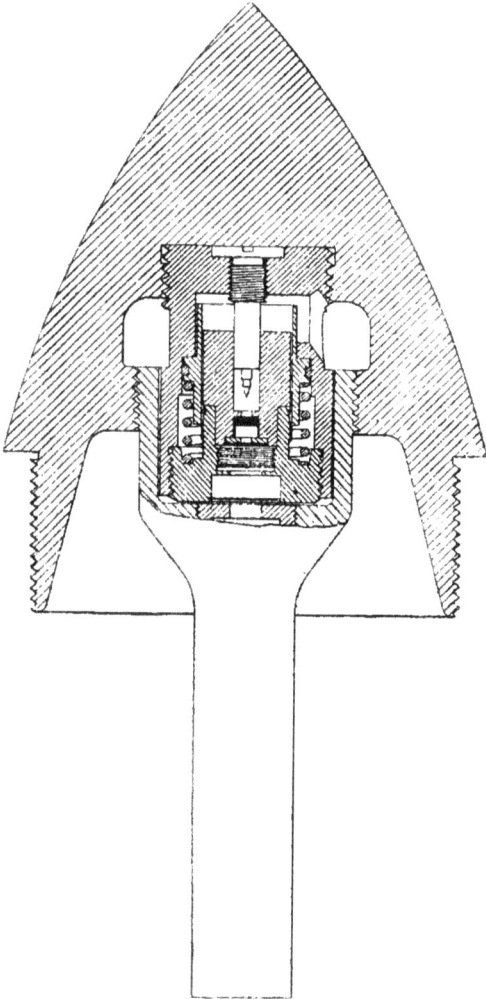

FIG. 7.

Internal percussion fuze in nose of shell for 10·4 cm. heavy gun.

1898 Pattern Base-Percussion Fuze.

Designation.—M. 98,

Used with—

6 cm. Gun (casemate mounting), 1898 and '99.
6 cm. Gun, 1898, in movable turret, with 1898 pattern shell.
Max. range, 1,500 metres.

Graduations.—None.

Material.—Brass.

Remarks.—

1898 Pattern Base-Percussion Fuze.

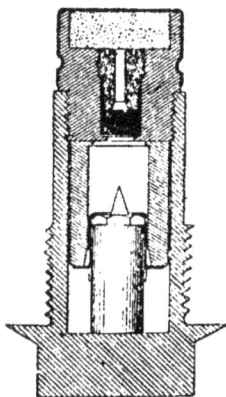

FIG. 8.

Base percussion fuze M. 8 used with 6 cm. fortress gun ('98 and '99), fixed or movable armoured mountings.

1909 Pattern Base-Percussion Fuze.

Designation.—M. 9 (10 cm., 15 cm. and 24 cm.).

Used with—

Ekrasit shell for—

10 cm. Mountain Howitzer, M. 99, 8, 10 and 16.

10 cm. Light Field Howitzer, 1899, and 14.

10 cm. Howitzer, M. 99, 5, 6 and 9, in cupola. Maximum range, 6,100 metres.

15 cm. Heavy Field Howitzer, 1894, '99, 94/4, 99/4 and 1914. Maximum range, with *Ekrasit* shell, M. 99/9, 5,600 metres.

24 cm. Mortar, '98 and '98/07, 95/10 and 10/16. Maximum range, 6,500 metres. (?)

Graduations.—None.

Material.—Brass.

Remarks.—M. 9, 15 cm., weighs 0·5 kilos. (1⅓ lbs.); M. 9., 24 cm., is larger, and weighs 1·7 kilos. (3¾ lbs.).

1909 Pattern Base-Percussion Fuze.

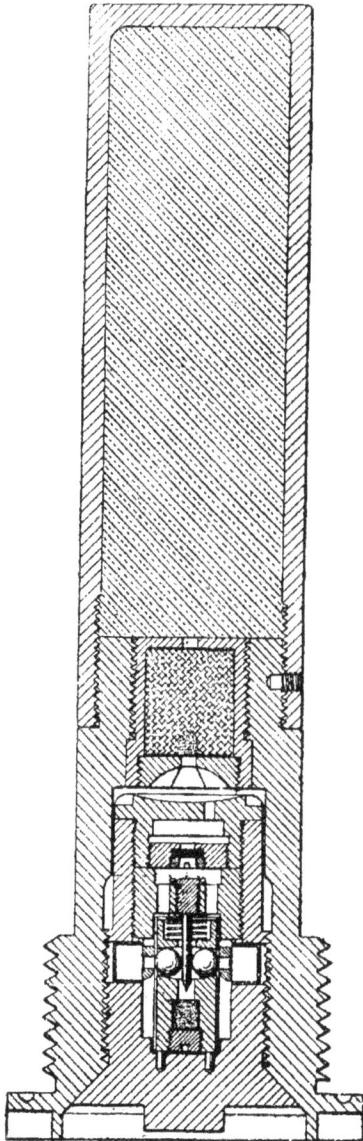

FIG. 9.

Base percussion fuze M. 9, with exploder, used with 24 cm. mortar.

Base Percussion Fuze for 30·5 cm. Shell.

Designation.—

    M. 9 (?) 30·5 cm.

Used with—30.5 cm. Mortar. Max. range, 12,800 metres.

Graduations.—None.

Material.—

    Remarks.—The fuze is borne on the base-plate of the shell, which is fuzed in two different ways. In earlier models the fuze was screwed down to a large plug, which in turn was screwed into the base-plate. For later model, *see* next page.

Base Percussion Fuze for 30·5 cm. Shell.

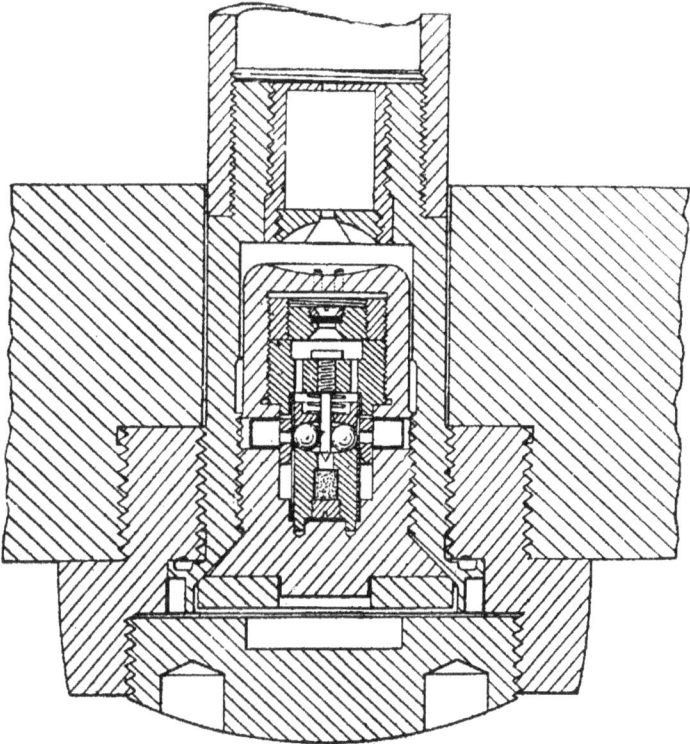

Fig. 10.

Base percussion fuze, for 30·5 cm. mortar. Earlier model, with fuze screwed down to a plug and the latter screwed into base-plate.

Base Percussion Fuze for 30·5 'um-gearbeitet' Shell.

Designation.—

    M. 9 (?) 30·5 cm.

Used with—30·5 cm. Mortar; *umgearbeitet* (*i.e.*, modified) shell
Max. range, 12,800 metres.

Graduations.—None.

Material.—

    Remarks.—The modified 30·5 cm. Shell has two base-plates ; the inner, and thicker, bears the fuze directly, with no plug ; the outer, and thinner base-plate is a flat disc completely closing the projectile. The object of this change was probably to prevent the infiltration of gas along the screw-threads of fuze and plug.

Base Percussion Fuze for 30·5 'um-gearbeitet' Shell.

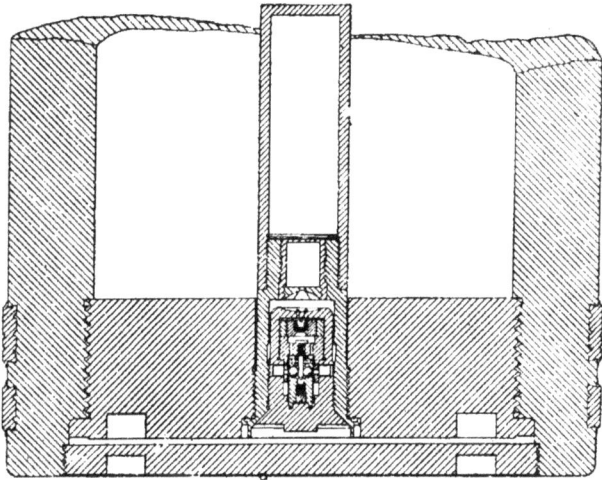

FIG. 11.

Base percussion fuze and exploder, for 30·5 cm. mortar. Later model : Shell with two base-plates and fuze screwed into the inner one.

Fuze for 38 cm. Gun.

Designation.—

Used with—38 cm. (Naval ?) Gun. Max. range said to be about 30 kilometers (18½ miles).

Graduations—

Material.—

Remarks.—A few 38 cm. Guns were employed by the Austrians in the Trentino offensive in May, 1916. Nothing is known of the fuze.

Fuze for 42 cm. Mortar.

Designation.—

Used with—42 cm. Mortar.   Range, 14,000 metres (?).

Graduations.—

Material.—

Remarks.—No details of fuze available.

41

1861 Pattern Time Fuze.

Designation.—M. 61.

Used with.—12 cm. and 15 cm. Guns (1861 and 61/95 models) forming part of mobile reserve of heavy artillery.

Graduations.—Nil.

Material.—

Remarks.—A primitive time fuze described by the Italian authorities. It consists of the mechanism for the ascent of the detonating needle and a wooden tube containing the composition. This is cut to a length corresponding to the time it is required to burn before being introduced into the body of the fuze.

This and the following old-fashioned fuzes were employed with projectiles made of cast iron with a jacket of lead. They were used by the Austrians in 1915-16 in the Val Camonica and Val Giudicaria, but have not been observed since then.

1866 Pattern Time Fuze.

Designation.—M. 66 and 66/85 k.

Used with.—

1866 and '78 shrapnel for :
12 cm. Gun ; 1861 and '61/95.   Max. range, 4,000 metres.
15 cm. Gun ; 1861 and '61/95.
(Mobile reserve of heavy artillery.)
15 cm. Mortar, 1878.   Max. range, 3,200 metres.

Graduations.—None.

Material.—M. 66 is made of *Zinnkupfer* (*i.e.*, copper with a small proportion of tin).

M. 66/85 K is of brass.

Remarks.—In both these fuzes the tube containing detonator-pellet is separate and is screwed into the fuze only just before the projectile is placed in the bore.

The letter " K " here shows the quality of powder in the composition (*i.e.*, *Kornpulver*).   It generally stands for *Kartätschschrapnell*, or case-shot.

1866 Pattern Time Fuze.

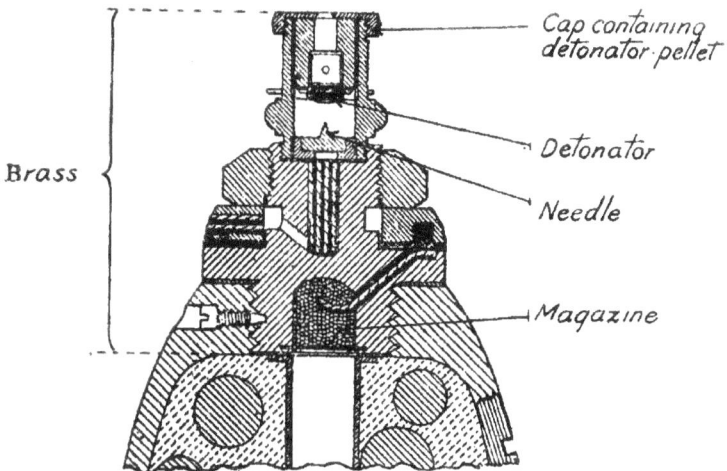

Fig. 12.

Ungraduated time fuze M. 66/85 K. in 1866 shrapnel, used by 12 cm. and 15 cm. guns of mobile reserve.

N.B.—" K." refers to the " time " composition (*see* opposite).

1875 Pattern Time Fuze.

Designation.—M. 75/85 c.

Used with.—8 cm. Guns (1895) in casemate mountings, with shrapnel 1875/85 c. pattern. Max. range, 2,500 metres.

Graduations.—From 5 to 48 in hundreds of paces. Every interval of 200 paces is shown by a number, and between the numbers are four graduations of 50 paces each.

There is no arrangement for case-shot effect.

Setting the fuze at the " 500 " mark produces a burst about 250 metres from the muzzle.

Material.—Brass.

Remarks.—Shrapnel employed with this fuze has a red " C " on the nose of the shell.

1875 Pattern Time Fuzes.

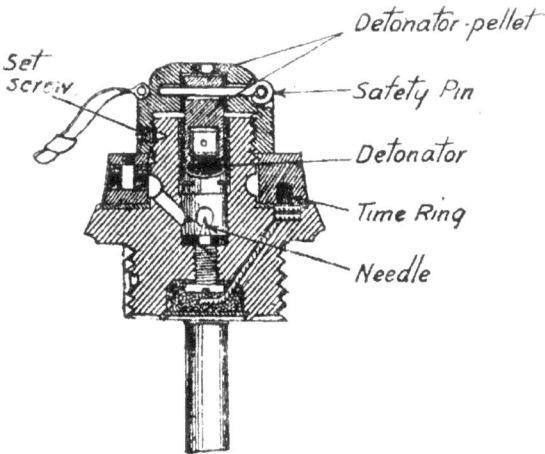

FIG. 13.

Graduated time fuze M. 75/85c for 8 cm. guns ('95 model), fixed armament.

1880 Pattern Time Fuze.

Designation.—M. 80 K.

Used with.—
1866 and '78 shrapnel for :
12 cm. Gun, 1861 and '61/95
15 cm. Gun, 1861 and '61/96.
(Mobile reserve of heavy artillery.)
15 cm. Mortar, 1878.

Graduations.—None.

Material.—Brass.

Remarks.—The detonator-pellet is united with the body of the fuze, but is prevented from moving before use by a safety-pin.
" K " indicates the nature of the composition (*i.e.*, *Kornpulver*).

1880 Pattern Time Fuze.

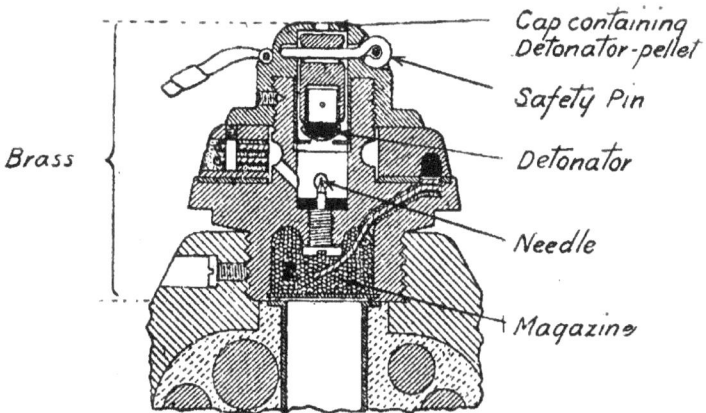

Cap containing
Detonator-pellet

Safety Pin

Detonator

Needle

Magazine

Brass

FIG. 14.

Ungraduated time fuze M. 80 K. in 1866 shrapnel, used by 12 cm.
and 15 cm. guns of mobile reserve.

N.B.—" K." refers to the " time " composition (*see* opposite).

1885 Pattern Time Fuzes.

Designation.—M. 85.

Used with.—8 cm. Field Gun, 1875 pattern, converted; with '75/85 shrapnel. Max. range, 3,375 metres.

Graduations.—Up to 45, in hundreds of paces. Each division equivalent to 200 paces is marked by a number, and between the numbers are four graduations of 50 paces each.

Material.—Brass.

Remarks.—

1891 Pattern Time and Percussion Fuze.

Designation.—M. 91 a, M. 91 b.

Used with.—

Shrapnel, M. 75/91 a and M. 75/91 b for :
9 cm. (old) Field Gun, 1875/96 ; max. range, **3,375** metres.
9 cm. Gun, 1875, '75/96, '75/04 and 1911 (?) (casemate mounting) ; max range, 3,375 metres.

Graduations.—From 6 to 48 in hundreds of paces. The graduation for every 200 paces bears a number, and the space between is subdivided into four divisions equivalent to 50 paces each.

Material.—Brass.

Remarks.—Set for percussion when the setting-mark is at " A " (*i.e.*, *Aufschlag*, percussion).

1893 Pattern Time and Percussion Fuze.

Designation.—M. 93 a.

Used with.—

Shrapnel, 1880 and '78 a pattern, for :
   12 cm. Heavy Gun, 1880 ; max. range, 6,500 metres.
   12 cm. Gun, 1880 and '96 in casemate or turret.
   15 cm. Heavy Field Howitzer, 1894, '99 and 1914 ; max.
      range, 5,000 metres.
   15 cm. howitzer in cupola.
   15 cm. Mortar, 1880, 98, 95/7 and 1916.
   15 cm. Mortar, 1878 (shrapnel 1878/93 a) ; max. range,
      3,200 metres.
   18 cm. Heavy Gun, 1880 ; max. range, 4,500 metres.
   15 cm. Heavy Gun, 1880 ; max. range, 8,500 metres.

Graduations.—From 0 to 25.   Each division is subdivided
into four.   When setting-mark is at " A " (*Aufschlag*), fuze is set
for percussion.

Material.—Bronze

Remarks.—The time of burning of the " time-composition " in
this fuze is comparatively short ; and allows time-shrapnel to be
used with it only up to ranges of 6,500 metres with 12 cm. and 15
cm. guns (1880), and up to 5,000 metres with 15 cm. Howitzers.
   To extend the range beyond these limits, an extra fuze, *Ergänzungszünder* (*see* next page) is screwed over the hexagon-cap.

	Max. Ranges with 1880/93 a Shrapnel.	
	Fuze M. 93 a.	93 a and *Er-gänzungszünder.*
	Metres.	Metres.
15 cm. Howitzer	5,000	5,900
12 cm. Gun	6,500	8,000
15 cm. Gun	6,500	8,500
18 cm. Gun	4,500	—
15 cm. Mortar....	3,200	—

1893 Pattern Time and Percussion Fuze.

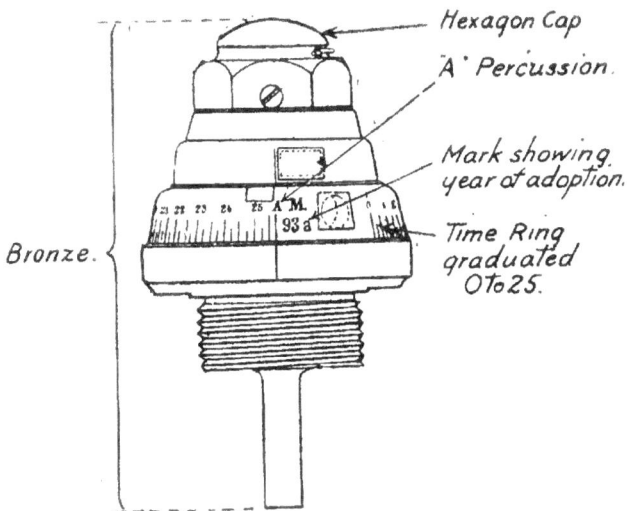

Hexagon Cap

'A' Percussion.

Mark showing year of adoption.

Time Ring graduated 0 to 25.

Bronze.

FIG. 15.

Time and percussion fuze M. 93A used with 12 cm., 15 cm. and 18 cm. heavy guns ; 15 cm. how. ; and 15 cm. mortar.

An extra fuze (*Ergänzungszünder*), to extend the time, is sometimes screwed over the hexagon cap (*see* next page).

" Ergänzungszünder " for 1893 Pattern Time and Percussion Fuze.

Designation.—*Ergänzungszünder* (*i.e.*, complementary fuze) M. 93 a, and M. 93 b.

Used with.—

1893-pattern time and percussion fuze (screwed over hexagon-cap), to extend range at which time-shrapnel may be fired with it.

M. 93 a for guns ; M. 93 b for Howitzers.

Graduations.—None.

Material.—Bronze ; originally aluminium.

Remarks.—The great variety of shrapnel of the three calibres, 12 cm., 15 cm., and 18 cm., fuzed with T. and P. fuze M. 93 a, does not always make it possible to tell, when the fuze only is found, to what projectile it belonged or what gun fired it.

But certain guides are available.

Thus, a T. and P. fuze M. 93 a, found with complementary fuze M. 93 b screwed on to it, certainly belongs to 1880/93 a shrapnel and was fired by a 15 cm. Howitzer. While a T. and P. fuze, M. 93 a, found with an *Ergänzungszünder* M. 93 a, certainly belongs to 1880/93 a shrapnel ; but was fired by a 12 cm. or 15 cm. heavy gun (1880 pattern). The 18 cm. gun cannot fire time-shrapnel at ranges long enough for the *Ergänzungszünder* to be necessary.

If the extra fuze is missing ; shell splinters coloured red indicate 15 cm. gun.

Again, if the interval between the sound of discharge and arrival of the shell is more than 11 seconds, a howitzer or mortar is firing ; if the interval is less than 11 seconds, it is probably a gun.

T. and P. fuze, M. 93 a.

1. If complementary fuze is present :
   - (*a*) Marked M. 93 b ... ... **15 cm. How.**
   - (*b*) Marked M. 93 a. :
     - (i) Nose of shell red ... ... **15 cm. Gun.**
     - (ii) Nose of shell not red ... ... **12 cm. Gun.**

2. If complementary fuze is missing :
   - (*a*) Nose of shell, red ... ... **15 cm. Gun.**
   - (*b*) Nose of shell not red :
     - (i) Interval between sound of discharge and arrival of shell *more* than 11 seconds ... **15 cm. How.** or **Mortar.**
     - (ii) Interval *less* than 11 seconds ... ... **12 cm. or 18 cm. Gun.**

" Ergänzungszünder " for 1893 Pattern Time and Percussion Fuze.

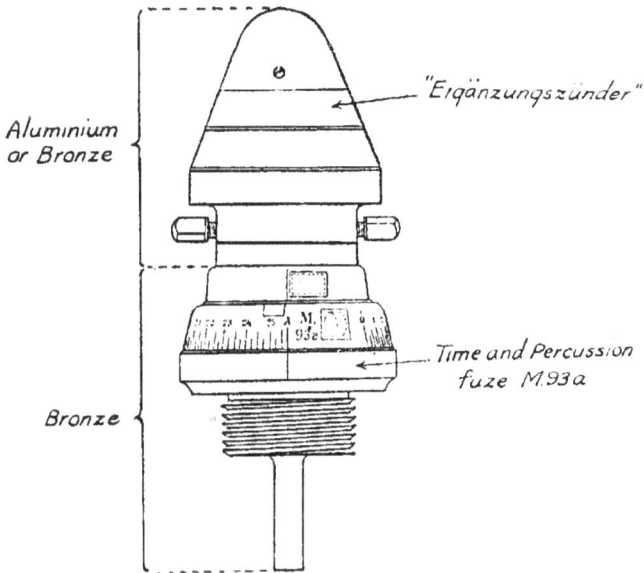

FIG. 16.

Ergänzungszünder, fitted on hexagon cap of time and percussion fuze M. 93A.

1895 Pattern Time and Percussion Fuze.

Designation.—M.'95.

Used with.—

Shrapnel M. 96/95 and 94/95.

8 cm. Gun in cupola (1894).

8 cm. Gun in casemate-mounting, 1894 and 1898.

8 cm. Fortress Gun on shielded carriage, 1894 ; max. range, 3,000 metres.

Graduations.—From 5 to 30 in hundreds of metres. Also a graduation for percussion ("A" *Aufschlag*); and one ("45") for a burst 450 metres from muzzle.

Material.—Brass.

Remarks.—

1895 Pattern Time and Percussion Fuze.

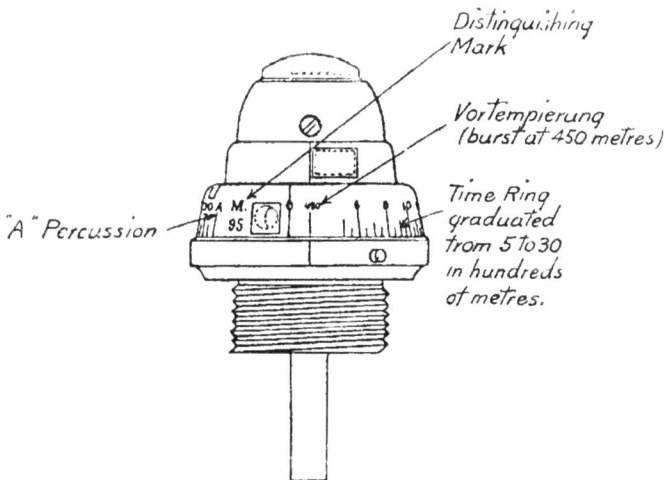

Distinguishing Mark

Vortempierung (burst at 450 metres)

Time Ring graduated from 5 to 30 in hundreds of metres.

"A" Percussion

FIG. 17.

Time and percussion fuze M. 95 used with 8 cm. guns, fixed armament.

1895/b Pattern Time and Percussion Fuze.

Designation.—M. 95 b.

Used with.—

Shrapnel, 98/95 b, for :
6 cm. Gun in casemate mounting, 1898.
6 cm. Gun in fixed or movable turret, 1898 ; max. range, 1,500 metres.

Graduations.—Up to 17, in hundreds of metres. Newer fuzes of this pattern have also a graduation " V " (*Vortempierung*) for bursts at about 200 metres from muzzle.

Material.—Brass.

Remarks.—

1896 Pattern Time and Percussion Fuze.

Designation.—M. 96, 96 a and 96 c.

Used with.—

Shrapnel, 1875, '91, '96, for :
  9 cm. (old) Field Gun, 1875, '75/96.
  9 cm. Gun in casemate mounting, 1875, '75/96, '75/04 and 1911 ;
    max. range, 4,500 metres.

Graduations.—From 6 to 48 in hundreds of paces. The graduation for every 200 paces bears a number, and the space between is subdivided into four divisions equivalent to 50 paces each.

The fuzes are set for percussion when setting-mark is at " A " (*Aufschlag*). M. 96 a and 96 c can also be set for case-shot effect at " K " (*Kartätschschrapnell*).

Material.—Brass.

Remarks.—

1896 Pattern Time and Percussion Fuze.

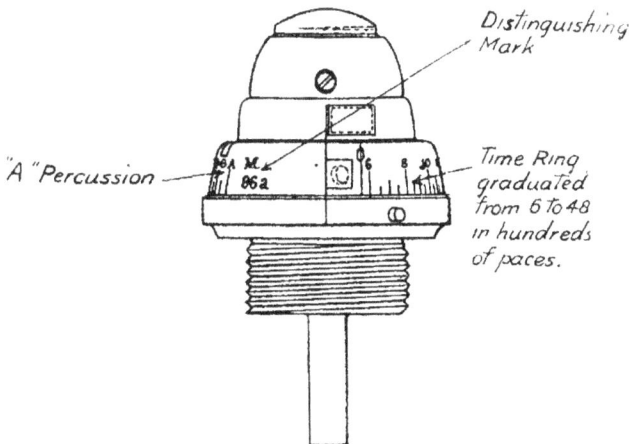

Fig. 18.

Time and percussion fuze M. 96A used with 9 cm. guns, fixed armament.

1899 7 cm. Time and Percussion Fuze.

Distinctive Mark.—M. 99, 7 cm.

Used with.—7 cm. Mountain Gun, 1899; 1908 and '9 for 1899 shrapnel; max. range, 4,000 metres (reckoned at sea-level), and 1905 *Ekrasit* shell; max. range, 5,300 metres.

Graduations.—Up to 40½ in hundreds of metres (*i.e.*, 4,050 metres of range). Smallest divisions represent 50 metres.

Other graduations are letters, V, K, A. When fuze is set at:

V. (*Vortempierung*), shrapnel bursts about 200 metres from muzzle.

K. (*Kartätschschrapnell*), bursts 5—10 metres from muzzle with case-shot effect.

A. (*Aufschlag*), bursts on percussion.

Material.—Brass.

Remarks.—Fitted with a gaine when applied to *Ekrasit* shells.

1899 7 cm. Time and Percussion Fuze.

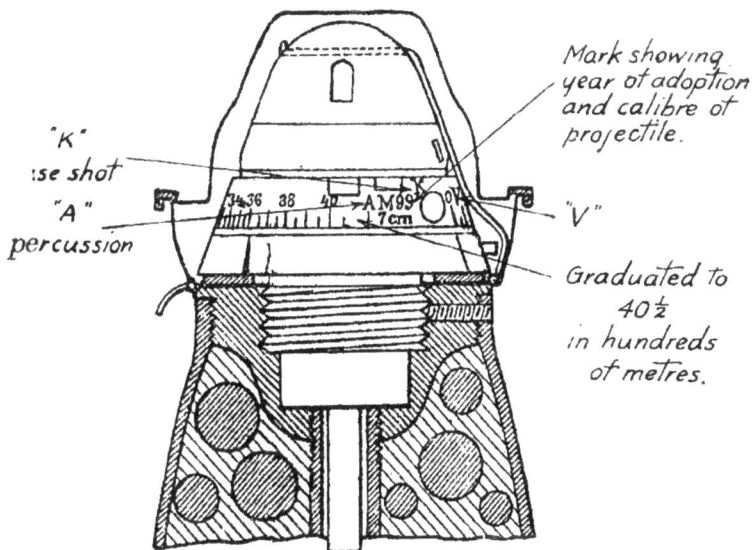

FIG. 19.

Time and percussion fuze M. 99 (7 cm.) in shrapnel of 7 cm. mountain gun (1899 model).

1899 10 cm. Time and Percussion Fuze, for Shrapnel.

Distinctive mark.—M. 99, 10 cm.

Used with.—

10 cm. Light Field Howitzer, 1899 and 1914.
10 cm. Mountain Howitzer, 1899, 1908, 10 and 16.
10 cm. Fortress Howitzer in cupola, 1899, 1905, '6 and '9.; max. range with shrapnel, 5,400 metres.

Graduations.—From 4 to 56 in hundreds of metres, only even numbers shown. (For letters V, K, and A, *see* previous page.)

Material.—Brass.

Remarks.—Differs from the corresponding fuze for *Ammonal* shell by :
1. Absence of a gaine.
2. Presence of a graduation " K." for case-shot effect.

(*See* next page).

1899 10 cm. Time and Percussion Fuze, for Shrapnel.

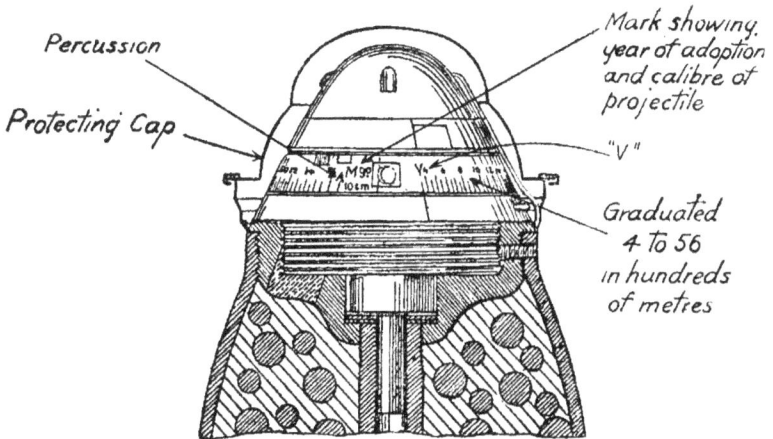

Percussion

Protecting Cap

Mark showing year of adoption and calibre of projectile

"V"

Graduated 4 To 56 in hundreds of metres

FIG. 20.

Time and percussion fuze M. 99 (10 cm.) in shrapnel from 10 cm. light field how. or 10 cm. mountain how.

1899 10 cm. Time and Percussion Fuze, for Shell.

Distinctive mark.—M. 99, 10 cm.

Used with.—
    10 cm. Light Field Howitzers, 1899, and 1914.
    10 cm. Mountain Howitzer, 1899, 1908, '10 and '16.
    10 cm. Fortress Howitzer in cupola, 1899, 1905, '6 and '9 ; max· range (with *ammonal* shell), 5,600 metres.

Graduations.—From 4 to 56 in hundreds of metres, only even numbers shown. (For letters V, and A, *see* page 68.)

Material.—Brass.

Remarks.—Differs from the 1899 pattern, 10 cm. fuze employed with shrapnel by :
    1. Having a gaine.
    2. Not having a graduation " K " for case-shot effect.

(*See* previous page.)

1899 a Pattern Time and Percussion Fuze.

Distinctive mark.—M. 99 a.

Used with.—

Star shell (*Leuchtschrapnell*) M. 6/99 a for :
15 cm. Heavy Field Howitzer, 1894, '99, 94/4, 99/4 and 1915.
15 cm. *Panzerhaubitze* (Howitzer in cupola), 1894, '99.
15 cm. Mortar. 1880, '98, '98/07, and 16.
15 cm. Mortar, in cupola, 1880, or on sledge.
21 cm. Coast defence Mortar, 1880, and Mortar, 1916.
24 cm. Mortar, 1880, '98 and '98/07, '95/10 and 10/15.

Graduations.—From 0 to 25 in hundreths of the length of the time-composition ; each division subdivided into four.

Material.—Brass.

Remarks.—

1899 a Pattern Time and Percussion Fuze.

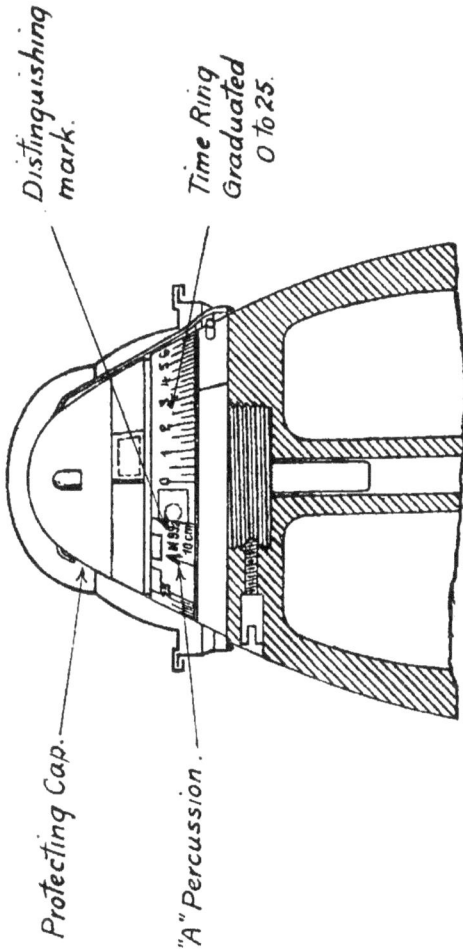

FIG. 21.

Time and percussion fuze M. 99A fitted to star-shell of 15 cm.
how. or mortar, or 21 cm. mortar.

1899 b Pattern Time and Percussion Fuze.

Distinctive mark.—M. 99 b.

Used with.—

Star-shell (*Leuchtschrapnell*) 6/99 b for :
10 cm. Light Field Howitzer, 1899 and 1914.
10 cm. Mountain Howitzer, 1899, 1908, 10 and 10.
10 cm. Fortress Howitzer (in cupola), 1899, 1905, '6 and '9.

Graduations.—From 0 to 25 in hundreths of the length of the time-composition ; each division subdivided into four.

Material.—Brass.

Remarks.—

1902 Pattern Time and Percussion Fuze.

Distinctive mark.—M. 2.

Used with.—8 cm. Q.F. Gun in turret, 1902 ; max. range with shrapnel, 4,000 metres.

Graduations.—

Material.—

Remarks.—

1905 Pattern Time and Percussion Fuze.

Distinctive Mark.—M. 5.

Used with—

8 cm. Field Gun, 1905 and 1905/8.

8 cm. Fortress Gun, 1905 and 1905/9.   Max. range : time, 6,200 metres ; percussion, 6,200 metres.

Graduations.—From 5 to 61 in hundreds of metres.   Each of the smaller divisions represents 50 metres.

Also letters V, A and K.   When fuze is set at—

V. (*Vortempierung*), shrapnel bursts about 200 metres from muzzle.

K. (*Kartätschschrapnell*), bursts 5-10 metres from muzzle, with case-shot effect.

A. (*Aufschlag*), bursts on percussion.

Material.—Bronze.

Remarks.—Fuze is set with a key, which engages in two slots on time-ring.

For use with Ammonal Shell, the fuze is fitted with a gaine.

It is being superseded by the following :—

1905 Pattern Time and Percussion Fuze.

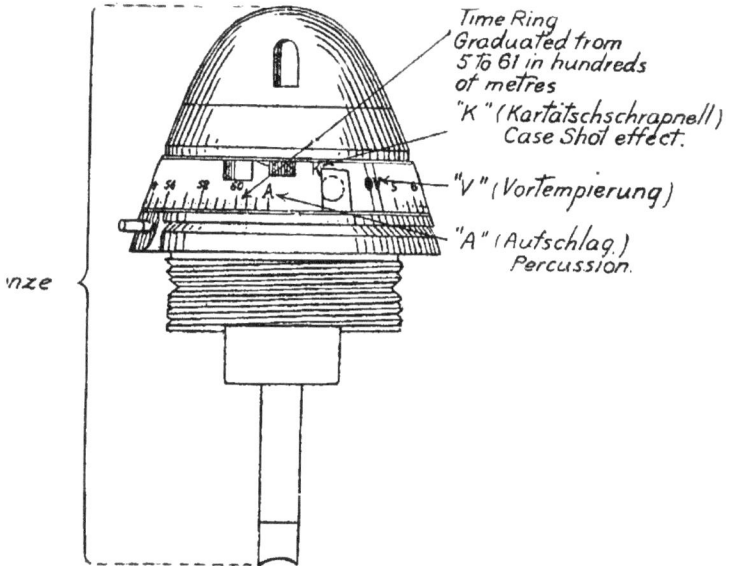

Time Ring
Graduated from
5 to 61 in hundreds
of metres

"K" (Kartätschschrapnell)
Case Shot effect.

"V" (Vortempierung)

"A" (Aufschlag.)
Percussion.

'nze

FIG. 22.

Time and percussion fuze M. 5. Bronze ; graduated to 61. Used with 8 cm. field gun.

Bronze 1908 Pattern Time and Percussion Fuze (No. 1).

Distinctive mark.—M. 8.

Used with—

8 cm. Field Gun, 1905 and 1905/8.

8 cm. Fortress Gun, 1905, 1905/9.   Max. range : time, 6,200 metres ; percussion, 7,000 metres.

Graduations.—From 5 to 61 in hundreds of metres.   (Later fuzes of 1908 pattern, are graduated as far as 73.)

Smaller divisions represent 50 metres each.

Letters V, K and A, as in 1905 pattern (*see* previous page).

Material.—Bronze.

Remarks.—Differs from the last by—

1. Distinguishing mark, M. 8 on time-ring.
2. Four pairs of studs on time-ring for setting by hand.
3. One circular hole, instead of 2 slots for setting key.
4. No detent pin.

Bronze 1908 Pattern Time and Percussion Fuze (No. 1).

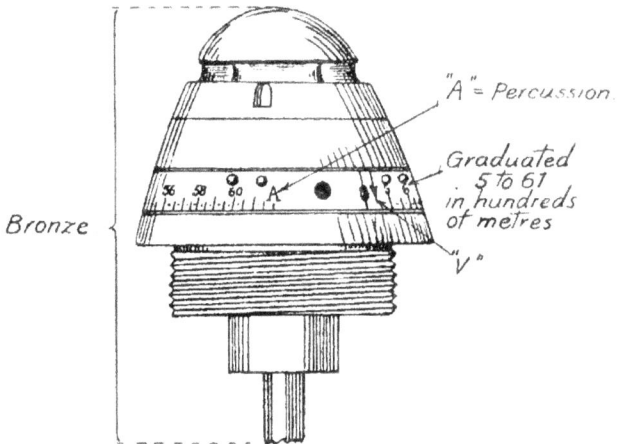

Fig. 23.

Time and percussion fuze M. 8. Bronze; graduated to 61. Used with 8 cm. field gun.

Bronze 1908 Pattern Time and Percussion Fuze (No. 2).

Distinctive mark.—M. 8.

Used with—

8 cm. Field Gun, 1905 and 1905/8.
8 cm. Fortress Gun, 1905 and 1905/8. Max. range (time an percussion), 7,300 metres.

Graduations.—From 5 to 73 in hundreds of metres. The small divisions represent 50 metres.

Letters V. A and K as in 1905 pattern fuze (page 80).

Material.—Bronze.

Remarks.—Set by hand (*Leichttempierbar*), using the four pai of studs on the time-ring.

With a gaine, this fuze is employed also for H.E. to get a time burst on targets behind cover.

Bronze 1908 Pattern Time and Percussion Fuze (No. 2).

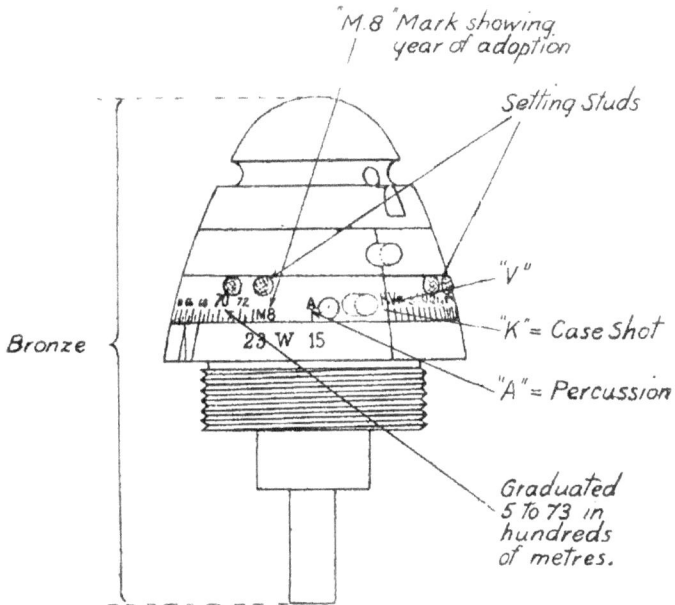

"M.8" Mark showing year of adoption

Setting Studs

"V"

"K" = Case Shot

"A" = Percussion

Bronze

23 W 15

Graduated 5 to 73 in hundreds of metres.

FIG. 24.

Time and percussion fuze M. 8; Bronze. graduated to 73. Used ith 8 cm. field gun.

Iron 1908 Pattern Time and Percussion Fuze.

Distinctive Mark.—M. 8.

Used with—

Shrapnel, M. 8, for—
8 cm. Field gun, 1905 and 1905/8.
8 cm. Fortress Gun, 1905 and 1905/8; Max. range, 7,300 metres.

Graduations.—From 5 to 73 in hundreds of metres. Smaller divisions, 50 metres.

Letters V, A and K as in 1905 pattern fuze.

Material.—Iron with brass ring.

Remarks.—Set by hand (*i.e.*, *Leichttempierbar*).

With a gaine, this fuze is employed also for H.E., to get a timed burst on targets behind cover.

Iron 1908 Pattern Time and Percussion Fuze.

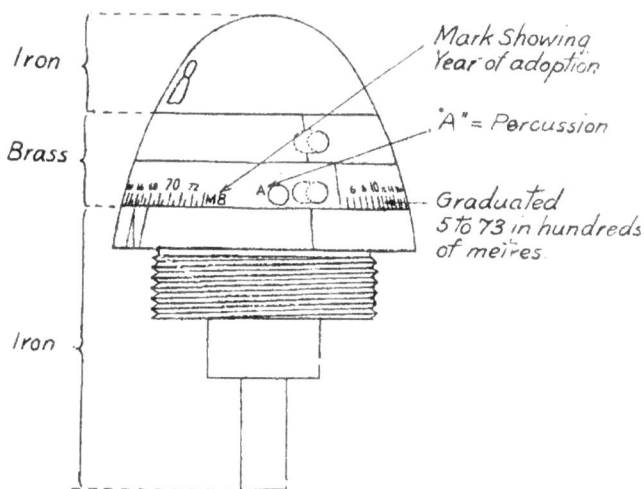

FIG. 25.

Time and percussion fuze M. 8. Iron, with brass rings ; graduated to 73. Used with 8 cm. field gun.

"Zusatzladung" Time and Percussion Fuze.

Distinctive mark.—M. 8 B. *Zusatzladung* (*i.e.*, additional charge).

Used with—

8 cm. Field Gun, 1905 and 1905/8.
8 cm. Fortress Gun, 1905 and 1905/8

Graduations.—Two independent scales :—

1. On lower (movable) time-ring, from 6 to 56 in hundreds of metres, each space representing 50 metres of range. The letters A, K and V have the same object as in 1905 and 1908 pattern T. and P. fuze.
2. On upper (fixed) ring, from 40 to 63 in hundreds of metres.

Material.—Rings, brass ; body of fuze, a leaden coloured alloy, covered with *Soehnée* varnish (looking rather like brass) to preserve it from oxidation.

Remarks.—This fuze was first employed against the Italians in 1916. The principle of it is new in the Austrian Field Artillery. The cartridge contains a reduced charge for ranges up to 5,600 metres ; an additional charge (*Zusatzladung*) brings the maximum range up to 6,300 metres. The fuze is separately graduated, by distance, for each charge. With the smaller charge, a more curved trajectory can be obtained, for use against targets behind cover ; and the wear of the gun is not so great. The full charge appears to be seldom used.

"Zusatzladung" Time and Percussion Fuze.

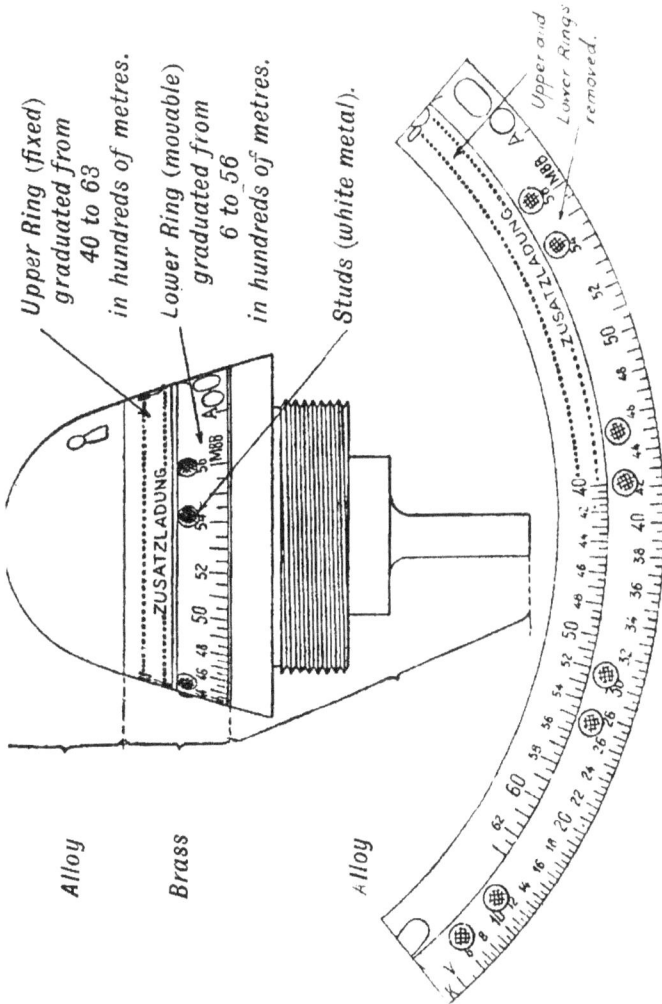

Upper Ring (fixed) graduated from 40 to 63 in hundreds of metres.

Lower Ring (movable) graduated from 6 to 56 in hundreds of metres.

Studs (white metal).

Upper and Lower Rings removed.

Alloy

Brass

Alloy

Time and percussion *Zusatzladung* fuze ; adapted for two charges ; used with 8 cm. field gun.

1912 Pattern Time and Percussion Fuze.

Distinctive Mark.—M. 12, on time-ring; either alone or followed by a letter to distinguish fuzes intended for different projectiles.

Used with—New ammunition (1912) for—

12 cm. Heavy Gun, 1880. Max. range, 6,500 metres.

12 cm. Gun, 1880 and '96 in casemate or turret.

15 cm. Heavy Field Howitzer, 1894, '99 and 1914. Max. range, 5,000 metres.

15 cm. Howitzer in cupola.

15 cm. Mortar, 1880, '98, 98/7 and 1916. Max. range, 3,200 metres.

15 cm. Mortar in cupola, 1880.

18 cm. Heavy Gun, 1880. Max. range, 4,500 metres.

Graduations.—5 to 61, in hundreds of metres.

" A " (*Aufschlag*), Percussion.

" K " (*Kartätschschrapnell*), case-shot.

" V " (*Vortempierung*), for burst about 300 metres from muzzle.

Material.—

Remarks.—This fuze and the three following belong to the new steel projectiles, which were brought out in 1912, to replace the cast-iron ammunition of the older fortress guns and howitzers.

With shrapnel, the fuze is screwed directly into the nose of the shell, with H.E. an iron gaine is fitted to the fuze, and an exploder then screwed to the bottom of it.

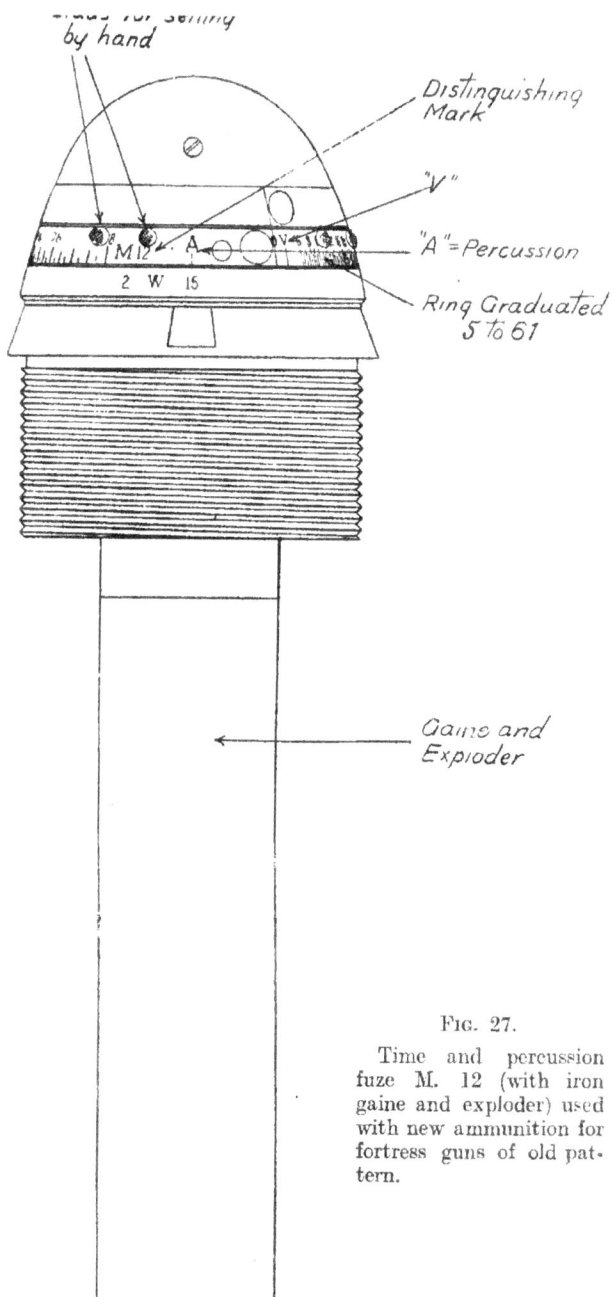

Studs for setting by hand

Distinguishing Mark

"V"

"A" = Percussion

Ring Graduated 5 to 61

M 12

2 W 15

Gaine and Exploder

FIG. 27.

Time and percussion fuze M. 12 (with iron gaine and exploder) used with new ammunition for fortress guns of old pattern.

1912 a Pattern Time and Percussion Fuze.

Distinctive Mark.—M. 12 a.

Used with.—New ammunition (1912) for :—

15 cm. Heavy Field Howitzer, 1894, '99, '94/04, '99/04 and 1915. Max. range, 5,000 metres.

15 cm. Howitzer in cupola.

15 cm. Mortar, 1880, '98, '98/07. Max. range, 3,200 metres.

15 cm. Mortar, 1880, in cupola.

Graduations.—

5 to 61, in hundreds of metres.

A, K. and V.

Material—

Remarks.—*See* previous page.

The fuze, as shown opposite, without gaine or exploder, would be used with shrapnel.

It is set by hand (*leichttempierbar*), using the four pairs of studs on the time-ring.

1912 a Pattern Time and Percussion Fuze.

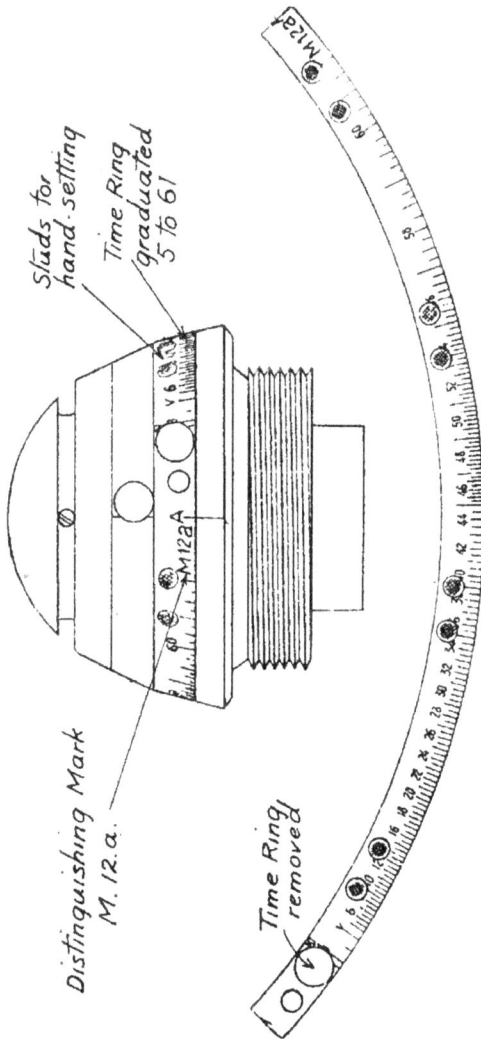

Studs for hand-setting

Time Ring graduated 5 to 61

M12aA

Distinguishing Mark M. 12. a.

Time Ring removed

Fig. 28.

Time and percussion fuze M. 12 a used with new ammunition for 15 cm. how. ('94 and '99 patterns).

1912 b Pattern Time and Percussion Fuze.

Distinctive Mark.—M. 12 b.

Used with.—New ammunition for :—

12 cm. Heavy Gun, 1880.   Max. range, 6,500 metres.
12 cm. Fortress Gun, 1880 and '96, in casemate or turret.
15 cm. Heavy Gun, 1880.

Graduations.—

6 to 84, in hundreds of metres.
A, K and V.

Material.—

Remarks.—*See* previous page.

1912 b Pattern Time and Percussion Fuze.

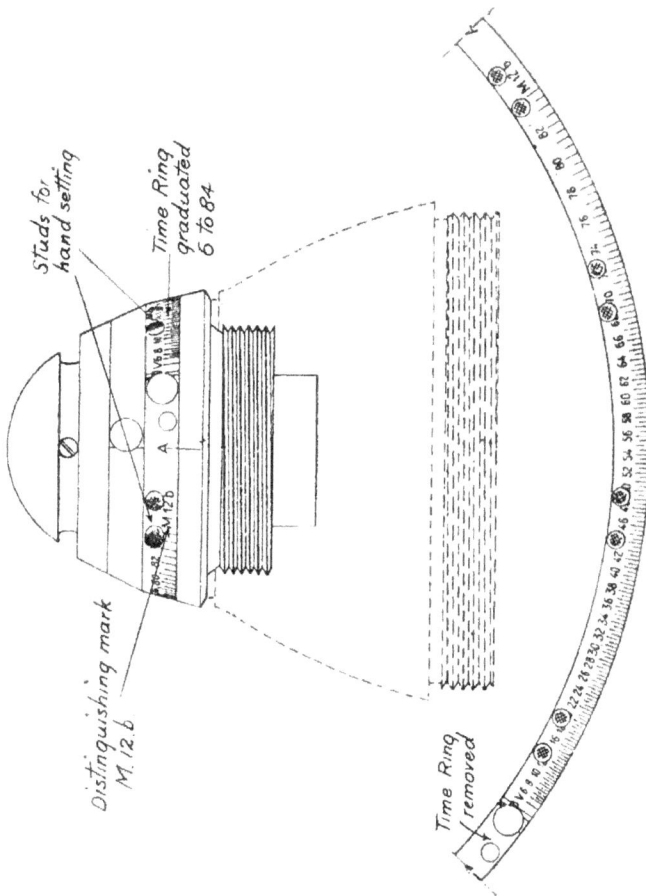

Studs for hand setting

Time Ring graduated 6 to 84

Distinguishing mark M. 12. b

Time Ring removed

Fig. 29.

Time and percussion fuze M. 12 b for new ammunition for 15 cm. gun (1880 pattern).

1912 f Pattern Time and Percussion Fuze.

Distinctive Mark.—M. 12 f.

Used with.—

Graduations.—

6 to 76, in hundreds of metres.
A, K and V.

Material.—

Remarks.—

1912 f Pattern Time and Percussion Fuze.

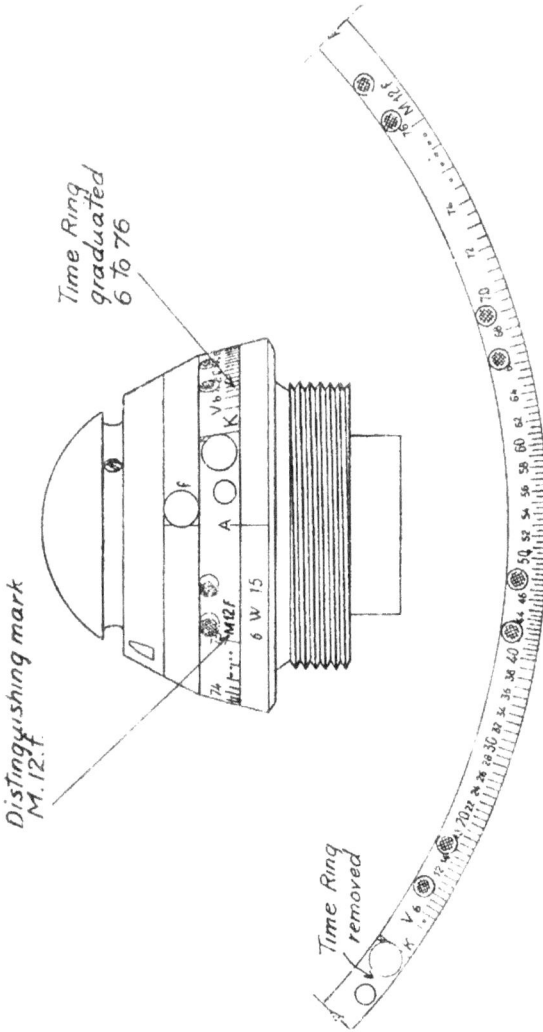

FIG. 30.

Time and percussion fuze M. 12 f used with new ammunition for gun or how. (?) of old pattern.

Time and Percussion Fuze for " Schrapnell-granate."

Distinctive Mark.—M. 14 (7 cm., 10 cm., or 15 cm.).

Used with.—" Universal shell " for :—

7·5 cm. Mountain Gun, 1915.

10·4 cm. Heavy Gun, 1914. Max. range, 12,500 metres.

15 cm. Heavy Field Howitzer, 1914. Max. range, 6,200 metres (?).

Graduations.—Up to 76 or 78 ; letters, A, K and V.

Material.—Bronze.

Remarks.—Similar to other T. and P. fuzes, except that, when set for *time*, the composition communicates the flash to the central tube, and thus to the magazine ; and when set for *percussion* the flash is communicated by a series of small holes to a circular chamber, filled with explosive, in the lower part of the fuze.

On bursting, the head of the shell, with the fuze attached, is violently separated from the rest of the projectile ; it continues on its way, and bursts on impact by the percussion mechanism of the fuze.

When the fuze is set at " A " (*Aufschlag*) for percussion, the whole thing goes off instantaneously on impact ; and the presence of a small charge of powerful explosive in the head increases the dispersal of bullets and splinters.

Time and Percussion Fuze for "Schrapnell-granate."

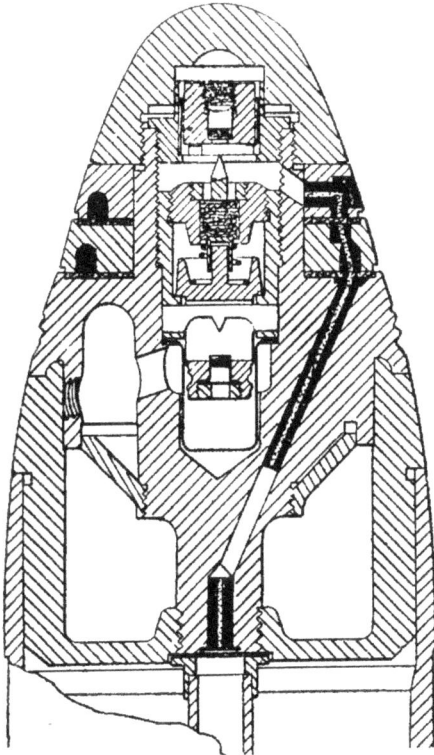

FIG. 31.

Time and percussion fuze, universal shell for 10·4 cm. gun (1914 pattern).

1892 Pattern German Time and Percussion Fuze.

Distinctive Mark.—Dopp. Z. 92, 10 cm. K. (*Doppel-Zünder*, 1892, *für* 10 *cm. Kanone, i.e.*, double-action fuze for 10-cm. gun).

Used with—10·4 cm. German Heavy Gun, K. 04. Max. range : time, 8,300 metres ; percussion, 10,500 metres.

Graduations.—From 1 to 26 in seconds and eighths of a second. When the setting mark is opposite the cross, the fuze is set for safety and will act only on percussion.

Material.—Brass.

Remarks —

1892 Pattern German Time and Percussion Fuze.

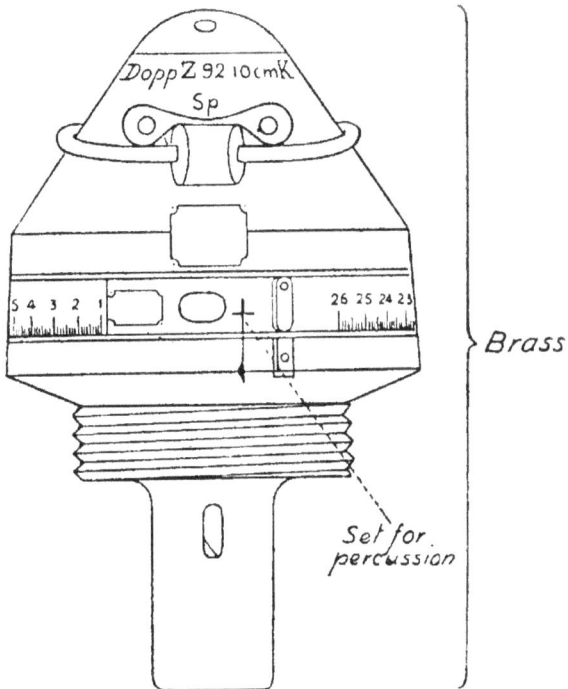

German time and percussion fuze (Dopp. Z. 92 f. 10 cm. K.) used with 10·4 cm. gun of German manufacture.

FIG. 33.

Nose of fuzed shell, with metal protecting cover over fuze,

ls.	Metres.	Metres.	Yards.	Inches.	Centimetres.	Centimetres.	Inches.
)0	12,801 ·	14,000	15,311 ·	36	91 ·44	36	14 ·17
)0	13,258 ·	14,500	15,858 ·	37	93 ·98	37	14. 57
)0	13,716 ·	15,000	16,404 ·	38	96 ·52	38	14 ·96
)0	14,173 ·	15,500	16,951 ·	39	99 ·06	39	15 ·35
)0	14,630 ·	16,000	17,498 ·	40	101 ·60	40	15 ·75
)0	15,087 ·	16,500	18,045 ·	41	104 ·14	41	16 ·14
)0	15,544 ·	17,000	18,592 ·	42	106 ·68	42	16 ·53
)0	16,002 ·	17,500	19,139 ·	43	109 ·22	43	16 ·93
)0	16,458 ·	18,000	19,685 ·	44	111 ·76	44	17 ·32
)0	16,916 ·	18,500	20,232 ·	45	114 ·30	45	17 ·71
)0	17,373 ·	19,000	20,779 ·	46	116 ·84	46	18 ·11
)0	17,830 ·	19,500	21,326 ·	47	119 ·38	47	18 ·50
)0	18,288 ·	20,000	21,873 ·	48	121 ·92	48	18 ·90
)0	18,745 ·	20,500	22,420 ·	49	124 ·46	49	19 ·29
)0	19,202 ·	21,000	22,966 ·	50	127 ·00	50	19 ·68

1 yard = 0·9143834 metres.
1 inch = 2·5399541 centimetres.
1 metre = 1·0936331 yards.
1 centimetre = 0·3937079 inches.

NAVAL & MILITARY

WWW.NAVAL-MILITARY-PREES.COM PRESS

THE GREAT WAR
TRAINING MANUALS, TEXT BOOKS
AND INSTRUCTIONS

On the outbreak of the Great War, the British Army was a small professional force of some 100,000 men. By the end of the conflict, after Kitchener's call for volunteers and finally conscription had scoured the nation for men, millions had served. To turn these civilians into soldiers, and to teach the new tactics and weapons that the war produced, the Army produced a hail of manuals, textbooks and instructions, many of which are available from the Naval and MIlitary Press.

9781474537384
TRENCH WARFARE

Notes On Attack And Defence February 1915 The manual strives to instil an offensive spirit and gives practical examples on: Close quarter, local, methods of successful warfare, and German attacks. The salient points to gather were preparation and co-operation between artillery and infantry, and that the capture of trenches is easier than their retention. Two plates illustrating tactics complete this official publication.

978147453581
Rapid Training of a Company for War

Reproduced from the 2nd and revised edition (in light of the most recent troop experiences, especially in the case of Engineering), "Rapid Training of a Company For War", was intended to be used by the junior officers in Kitchen's New Army to bring raw recruits efficiently,and in the shortest time available ,to be physically fit,and able to march and fight.

9781783313686
HANDBOOK OF FIREWORK AND SIGNALLING STORES IN USE BY LAND, NAVAL AND AIR SERVICES 1920

Covered in this corrected to January 1920 SECRET handbook are Bombs, Cartridges, Flares, Grenades, Rockets, Signals etc. With 73 clear technical line drawing plates, this is a very good official guide to signalling ordnance, much of which was in service during the Great War.

9781783313747
MILITARY ENGINEERING MINING AND DEMOLITIONS (GENERAL STAFF, 1915)

An important official publication covering all aspects of subterranean warfare with much practical detail for the guidance of mining companies of the Great War.

9781783310180
TRENCH FORTIFICATIONS 1914-1918. A Reference Manual

This is a compilation on the subject of trench warfare fortifications as taught by three national Armies - French, German and American. It is designed to give the enthusiast and scholar some idea of field engineering tasks on the Western Front during the Great War.

9781847348562
Hand Grenades: A Handbook on Rifle and Hand Grenades. 1917

Written by a serving officer, this handbook aims to give a complete knowledge of grenades in use during the Great War. Describing the use and effects of grenades in clear terms, the author aims to give the reader a quick grasp of grenades and the tactics involved in their employment.

9781847348210
Notes for Infantry Officers on Trench Warfare, March 1916

This exceptionally important official handbook was the Bible for infantry officers on the western front in the Great War. It covers a wealth of subjects essential to the efficient conduct of trench warfare, which, although published as late as March 1916, it still insists is only a temporary phase.An absolutely indispensible volume for anyone interested in the Great War.

9781474537971
THE OFFENSIVE OF SMALL UNITS
September 1916

This is a periodical tactical manual from 1916, it focuses on the manner in which the French organised and executed their attacks and counterattacks . Summarised from the French, it lays out the process by which to operate in attacks on the German trenches. Focused purely on the operation of infantry, the purpose of this British translation is to give small infantry units the benefit of the French experience in regard to the best methods of combat, in offensive operations.

9781783313761
ROYAL LABORATORIES HANDBOOK OF AMMUNITION
May 1918

For the use of Battery Commanders to give detailed guidance on the current types of ammunition in use. This periodic publication was not to be taken into first line trenches due to its confidential content. With clear colour technical drawings and comprehensive descriptions throughout, this is a must for those with an in interest in Great War ordnance, especially that used in the latter part of the War.

9781783315673
DEFENSIVE MEASURES AGAINST GAS ATTACKS 1917

Gas was a very effective way of attacking the enemy without direct contact, and attacks were the thing soldiers in the trenches feared over anything. This manual originally published by the War Office in February 1917, covers topics including the nature of gas: attacks, types, projectiles, personal anti-gas equipment & general precautions & observations.